Lord, Teach Us to Pray

Sermons on the Lord's Prayer

David A. Davis

Scripture quotations from the New Revised Standard Version of the
Bible are copyright (c) 1989 by the Division of Christian Education of
the National Council of Churches of Christ in the U.S.A. and are used by
permission.

Published by:
    Clear Faith Publishing, LLC
    22 Lafayette Road
    Princeton, NJ 08540

ISBN 978-1-940414-05-8

Printed in the United States of America

First Printing October, 2015
Cover and Interior Design by Doug Cordes
Lord, Teach Us to Pray is typeset in Verb and Paperback

Table of Contents

Dedicated to the loving memory of

William C. Barger

and

David D. Prince

mentors, colleagues, friends
who spent their lives proclaiming the
gospel in word and in deed

D.A.D. Fall 2015

Foreword

Welcome to this sermon series that offers you a window into the life of Nassau Presbyterian Church in Princeton, New Jersey, situated on Palmer Square and thus, as Dave Davis often reminds us, "in the heart of town and physically adjacent to Princeton University." In this space Nassau's congregational life and witness gives glory to God as it cares for the life of the heart and mind and for the life of the world in Princeton, in Trenton (a very different community just down the road, where we have partnerships), and in places as far-flung as Guatemala, Myanmar, and Nepal.

These 2015 Lenten sermons on the Lord's Prayer were offered alongside a church-wide small group discussion of the phrases of the prayer Jesus gave us, so members could reflect on the familiar prayer in corporate study as well as in worship. Members of the senior high group studied the prayer and several of them prepared short sermons on "daily bread" for Youth Sunday that are included in this volume. Four Eastertide sermons on the four gospel resurrection accounts expanded our reflection on the conclusion of the prayer. Nassau seeks to be a more and more open and welcoming congregation, and as one small sign of welcome, Sunday by Sunday those gathered for worship are encouraged to pray the prayer in the language and version closest to their own heart.

Over the fifteen years that Dave Davis has served as Nassau's pastor, there has developed what might be called an unwritten but much valued "covenant of expectations" about the range of content of his sermons. First, Scripture will have a central place in the sermon. Although that might sound self-evident, the key word is "central"; the biblical text is never just a springboard for something else.

Second, the world and its concerns are not left aside in the preaching life of this congregation. Nassau welcomes all, and its membership is diverse in its theological and political perspectives, but this does not mean that difficult issues in the news media are left at the door. In this regard Nassau's preaching life differs from that of many congregations, regardless of where they may place themselves on a theological spectrum. As you read these sermons, notice how "current events," issues of violence and intolerance, race, poverty, and division in the body politic nationally and globally, are incorporated into the congregation's community discourse. People talk to Dave at the door, or by email or phone, and equally important, they also they talk to one another. Week by week, sermons model for us how as Christians we can grapple with hard issues in the light of our faith, not as if in a separate realm.

For some readers, these sermons will provide an opportunity to slow down and reflect on the craft or structuring of sermons. While always central, Scripture is presented in differing ways, even as the sermons are developed in varying ways. Observe, for example, the openings. One sermon may begin with a series of single verses or phrases from various parts of Scripture. Another begins with a retelling or review of the text just read. Another begins with phrases evoking a particular emotion in different aspects of our daily life. Another begins with a single contemporary story, while yet another begins with several personal stories—and the connection among them emerges only in an unexpected tie to the biblical text for the morning. But always the connection to the biblical text becomes clear; there are no illustrations "for the sake of illustration," just to keep the congregation paying attention. In sum, the text of the day is itself always in one sense or another the core illustration for the sermon. Sometimes that happens through close attention to a single word— whether through sharing a debate over translation, or the range of meanings in Greek, or commentators' efforts to make sense of an unusual word. Sometimes it happens through a retelling of the biblical narrative or parable so as to embed it more deeply in the hearers. And depending on where that retelling is situated in the sermon and how it is worded, it can carry overtones of contemporary issues without overt reference. Watch, for example for the appearance of cell-phone pictures in the retelling of the parable of the king and the unforgiving servant (Lent V, Matt 18:21-35).

The illustrations in these sermons work because Dave is a gifted storyteller who can create the scene. Note, for example, the small reference to "a lamp with pull chain" on a lectern that sets the scene in a funeral home. Notice how even seemingly "academic" information about Greek words or about debating commentators or about variation in gospel accounts is incorporated in a "story-telling" way, illustrating some aspect of the church's journey of faith. But in the end, how well the illustrations are crafted is not the most important point. What is most important, important *theologically*, is that the stories are real, not made up. As Jesus used situations from the everyday life to teach his disciples, so Dave has a gift for discerning God's presence in what appears to be so very ordinary all around us. As the congregation hears such examples Sunday after Sunday, we are helped to grow in our own ability to reflect on God's presence in the "little things" as we live in faith, hope, and love.

As I have read and re-read these sermons I have found myself once again brought into the presence of the Holy One in a way that evokes a response that is for me not only spiritual or intellectual, but actually visceral. Will that happen for the reader who is not part of Nassau's worshiping community, who has not listened to podcasts or cannot quite catch in the mind's ear the cadence of the words? I pray that in the power of God's Spirit every reader will be encouraged, challenged, blessed, and transformed by what Dave Davis shares here.

Katharine Doob Sakenfeld

Nassau Congregant, Professor Emerita
Princeton Theological Seminary

"Our Father, Who Art in Heaven"

Pray then in this way: Our Father in heaven, hallowed be your name. Your kingdom come. Your will be done, on earth as it is in heaven. Give us this day our daily bread. And forgive us our debts, as we also have forgiven our debtors. And do not bring us to the time of trial, but rescue us from the evil one.

Way before I was born, my father played professional football. When I started to play, he taught me some things that the coaches never did. Like … almost all of the time, a quarterback is going to subconsciously look in the direction that the play will go before the ball is hiked; you can tell by the pressure a lineman puts on his hands whether the play will be a run or a pass; the person hiking the ball always grabs tighter right before the snap. Each of these small tidbits helped me make quite a few plays back in the day. Often right in the moment, or maybe after the game in the locker room, or now years later when I remember, it makes me think of my Dad and how he taught me.

In the first few months after I was ordained, I was visited in my office at the church by a retired pastor whose name was Ed. At that time, he had been retired longer than I had been alive. Ed gave me a whole bunch of advice that morning. One piece was this, "David, you will always have to work at understanding the church budget, money, and stewardship as well as the treasurer, the finance chair, or members of session. They don't realize it, but most church members would prefer their pastor not understand anything about money, in general, and the church finances, in particular. That way they can more easily live by the myth that their faith and their money don't go together. Your job as a spiritual leader is to correct them every week. And it starts by letting them know you understand the church's financial picture better than they do." Whenever I work at understanding a financial statement or prepare a budget or preach stewardship, I remember that old pastor; how he taught me.

When my wife and I were first married, my mother prepared a small notebook with 3x5 cards that had recipes on them. Almost 30 years later, we still use them. The most important recipe there is the secret Davis family barbeque sauce recipe, made available to others only by marriage. You would think I could make that recipe from memory by now, and I probably could. But I always look for the book. I pull out the book and I read the card, not so much for the recipe but because it is in my mother's handwriting. Every time I make that sauce, I do it with gratitude in my heart for my mom, remembering how she taught me.

Jesus said, *"Pray then like this." "Whenever you pray,"* don't be like those who like to be seen. *"Whenever you pray,"* go into your room and shut the door, and pray to your Father who is in secret. *"When you are praying,"* do not heap up empty phrases; your Father knows what you need before you ask. *"Pray then like this."* Jesus said that whenever you pray, when you are praying, and pray then like this: *"Our Father in heaven."*

When offering his commentary on the Lord's Prayer in his *Institutes of the Christian Religion*, John Calvin points out that whenever you call God "Father," whenever you pray to God as "Father," you are really just praying in the name of Christ. Who else, why else, would you dare to call God "Father." "Who would break forth into such rashness," Calvin writes, "as to claim for [themselves] the honor of a [child] of God unless we have been adopted as children of grace in Christ." To pray to God as Father is to "put forward" the name of Christ.

To pray the Lord's Prayer, to begin the Lord's Prayer, it is to remember and offer gratitude for the one who taught us to pray, the one in whom we know ourselves to be God's children, for so we are. Should we have a conversation about the multiple images for God in scripture? Certainly. In the 16th century, Calvin was quoting scripture from Isaiah 49, citing the motherhood of God. Should we affirm together God that is beyond gender? No question. Of course, most are comfortable affirming God has no gender, until someone refers to God as "her" or "she." Should we offer a theological conviction on the personhood of God, that language and image is the only way we have which enables us to name a God of relationship, a God for us, a God with us? Of course. Should we offer space for a pastoral reality check that acknowledges the baggage, the hurt, the grief, and the pain that can come with the term "father" for so many? Yes!

But when you pray, specifically the Lord's Prayer, perhaps Calvin is correct that to pray "Our Father" is not just a way of invoking God, but a means of allowing the heart to think afresh on Jesus and our life in him? *"Pray then like this."* Every time you pray "Our Father" it is a time to remember Christ Jesus and to affirm that "*neither death, nor life, nor angels, nor rulers, nor things present, nor things to come, nor powers, nor height, nor depth, nor anything else in all creation, will be able to separate us from the love of God in Christ Jesus our Lord.*" The God we know and experience in Christ Jesus, our Lord. *Our Father.* Remember how he taught us.

Anne Lamott, in her short book *Help, Thanks, Wow: The Three Essential Prayers*, refers to the Lord's Prayer as one of the "beautiful pre-assembled prayers." She compares it to one of the prayers of Thomas Merton, or the 23rd Psalm. Prayers like that "have saved me more times than I can remember," Lamott writes. "But they are for special occasions. They are dressier prayers, the good china of prayers." Useful, she argues, when you have enough wits about you to remember, and when you can find yourself entering into enough of a state of trust to even say them. "This would be approximately seven percent of the time," she concludes. Meaning, that for Anne Lamott, some other form of prayer is what kicks in 93% of the time.

By her own description in the book on prayer, she acknowledges that her family never prayed when she was growing up. People who prayed were ignorant, and her parents were "too hip and intellectual to pray." I don't know about you, but my experience of the Lord's Prayer is different from Anne Lamott's. Growing up in the Church and serving as a pastor all these years, it's not a "good china" experience. It's more like that serving dish passed on from your grandmother that you would be absolutely crushed if someone broke while doing the dishes. The Lord's Prayer; it's so deep inside. The Lord's Prayer at the front of the church with a couple getting married. The Lord's Prayer at a hospital bedside with a family. The Lord's Prayer in the cemetery. The Lord's Prayer in a continuing care room. The Lord's Prayer with a mom whose newborn is at her breast. The Lord's Prayer before a Bible study. The Lord's Prayer with second graders. The Lord's Prayer after choir practice. The Lord's Prayer on your knees with your child. The Lord's Prayer in bed that first night of college. The Lord's Prayer somewhere overseas when you were in the service. The Lord's Prayer here in worship. Even the "nones," the non-practicing folks, when life is a flutter it's the Lord's Prayer that gets said. Far more than 7% of the time and something much different than "the good china of prayers." And it all starts with *"Our Father, who art in heaven."* Remember how Jesus taught us.

Our Father. Sometimes I wonder if the prayer couldn't stop right there. If there are not times when it does stop right there. *Our Father.* Like in an airport when you are waiting to see a loved one who has not been home for such a long time. You start to speak, "Oh, Sweetie…" and nothing else comes out but an embrace. Like when your child experiences the heartbreak of a first break-up, or not making the musical, or getting cut from the team and you start to speak, "Oh Charlie, Oh, Christy…" and you really have no words to say much more. Like when a friend tells you she's pregnant, or they just got a job, or they passed their oral exam…you shout their name and scream a bit, and what's more to say. Like when you walk into the room to offer an embrace to someone whose heart is broken with grief.

To call on, to invoke, to speak, to shout, to weep. To start a prayer and it stops at something like a sigh. *"Our Father,"* like Jesus taught us. Holding your newborn babe in your arms for the first time, encircled there in the room. Someone starts it, *"Our Father, who art in heaven,"* and you just can't finish as the tears of joy drip on the receiving blanket. To watch on the news and learn of the Christians brutally murdered by ISIS in Libya, and to know nothing else to say or pray than just *"Our Father,"* or to read the letter Kayla Mueller wrote to her family in the spring of last year. Before she was killed by those who held her hostage, she wrote about her love for her family, and her trust in God. You read it, and no words come. You stare at your computer, at the screen, praying for her, for her family, for this blasted world, and the whole mess, wondering, asking, pleading; where can this all go? But all you can muster is *"Our Father."* You sit here in the sanctuary on any given Sunday with a heart so heavy with concern or so relieved with joy that all you can say is *"Our Father"* and let the rest of us finish the prayer! "God, Our Father" is more than a way to start. It's a prayer all by itself. Sometimes it's all you can get. A sigh. A gasp. A prayer. Like Jesus taught us.

Not long ago, I was working with a family to prepare for a memorial service for their mother, grandmother, mother-in-law. One of the memories that I won't forget had to do with her mealtime table, and the memories they had of sharing a meal together at mother's table. They told me whether you were having just a sandwich, or breakfast, or more of a holiday meal, the table was always set; placemat, napkin, simple dishes, nothing fancy. The place setting reminded them of her welcome, her hospitality, and how she could make the little things so important. The table was always set. And it told them of her love.

Some tables, some meals, go so far beyond words. The Lord's Table tells of God's love. When you settle in at this table, sometimes just being here is a prayer. Remembering how he taught us. *Our Father, who art in heaven.*

"Hallowed Be Thy Name"

Hebrews 12:28-29

LENT II

*Therefore, since we are receiving a kingdom that
cannot be shaken, let us give thanks, by which we offer
to God an acceptable worship with reverence and awe;
for indeed, our God is a consuming fire.*

Hallowed. Hallow-ed. In the Lord's Prayer, as it appears
in the Greek of the New Testament, the word *hallowed*
is a verbal form of the root word for "holy." "Holy" is a
descriptor, an adjective. *Hallow* is a verb, an action word.
Hallow: to make holy, to sanctify, to purify. Hallowed. Sanctified. Purified. *Hallowed be Thy name.* Sanctified. Purified.
Hallowed is your name, O God. God's name is holy. Yes.
God is holy. But the phrase in the prayer connotes action;
it comes in a verbal form. God is not just holy. Not just
your name is holy, O God. But make holy, keep holy your
name. Maybe we just have to make up a word, how about
"holy-fy"? "Holy-fy" your name. Holy. Precious. Awesome.
Awesome-ify your name, O God.

Not just the descriptor, but the action. Hallowed. Sanctified. Purified. Holy-fied. One might conclude that the
action, here, the bestowing of holiness on God comes
from the person offering the prayer. That you and I
somehow keep God holy, make God holy, maintain God's

holiness as the words take shape on our lips. I had a coach in college who had a favorite saying when one of us would make a mistake. He said it often, with great volume, and in the strongest of Boston accents: "Holy Mary, Mother of God!" I can pretty much guarantee that Mary was no more holier because of him. In the biggest of pictures, in the grand theological scheme, it stands as fairly obvious that humanity is not in the business of preserving the holiness of God, even by our most pious efforts. No, the action implied, acknowledged here at the beginning of the Lord's Prayer, it must belong to God. *Hallowed* be Thy name.

Holy places. Holy moments. Holy people. Holy things. Your list might be long. Your list might be short. But everyone has a list of what they consider holy in their lives. People whisper in holy places. People get goose bumps, or get teary, or speechless in holy moments. People honor and are humbled by those they consider holy. People handle and preserve, and shine and dust holy things. If you took your list of that which is holy in your life and tried to use other words, other descriptors, think what those words would be: special, memorable, unique, faith-filled, unforgettable, sacred, godly, loveable, irreplaceable, important, priceless. It's kind of odd, the word "holy" is so overdone and can be so easily trite. Yet, other words really won't do. When it comes to trying to grasp what on earth, or in heaven, it means that God is holy, none of those other words on the list even come close. When you're trying to find meaning in the biblical witness to the holiness of God, words don't come all that easy. When you're trying to make any sense in your own life to what difference it makes that God is holy, all those other words just sort of fall into a heap of "not very helpful." When you and I pray, *"hallowed be Thy name," "holy is your name, O God,"* it sort of serves as an acknowledgment that nothing else really works. It's the best we can do. It's the only language we have for you, O God.

Our Lenten Small Groups, who are reflecting on and discussing the Lord's Prayer, are using a study guide offered through the website called "The Thoughtful Christian." A Methodist pastor and professor wrote the study guide for each week. In addressing *"hallowed be Thy name,"* the author points out the tension between the intimacy of calling God "Father" and the distance implied with "hallowed." He goes on to point out how that tension portrays the immanence and the transcendence of God. *Immanence* meaning "God present with us." *Transcendence* asserting that God is far beyond us. Here in the opening phrase, the writer concludes, "The immanence and the transcendence of God are equally true and equally important, each so true that their concepts must be blended in one breath."

Here's the problem, immanence and transcendence, that might be good for conversation on a cold night in a warm living room with coffee and a bun, it might be good for study and writing and discussion in a classroom down the street, it's just not very helpful when you are actually praying the Lord's Prayer. When you are saying the prayer just before sleep that you have said as long as you can remember, when you have climbed to the top of a mountain on a crisp summer day and creation so knocks your socks off that you have no other words to say, when you are in the waiting room and so anxious you can't really think of anything else, when you are craving a relevant and compelling notion about God, when you are praying *"hallowed be Thy name"* you are not thinking about immanence and transcendence. Keep on being holy, O God. Now, right now, O God, preserve your holiness in my life and in your world.

Don't stop being holy, Lord God. Because, as one preacher, the preacher in the Book of Hebrews, puts it: *Our God is a consuming fire.* *"Since we are receiving a kingdom that cannot be shaken, let us give thanks by which we offer to God an acceptable worship with reverence and awe; for indeed, our God is a consuming fire."* A consuming fire. Well, that's hardly a domesticated, overdone understanding of holy; God is a consuming fire. Commentators point out that the Book of Hebrews is to be read, understood, and heard as a sermon. The sermon is from an unknown preacher that heralds the work of Christ Jesus as the great high priest who was sacrificed at the cross for us. *"Long ago God spoke to our ancestors in many and various ways by the prophets, but in these last days God has spoken to us by a Son (1:1)."* That's how the sermon (the letter of Hebrews) begins. Memorable verses are throughout. *"Let us, therefore, boldly approach the throne of grace with boldness, so that we may receive mercy ... Let us hold fast to the confession of our hope without wavering ... and let us provoke one another to love and good deeds ... Now faith is the assurance of things hoped for, the conviction of things not seen ... Therefore, since we are surrounded by so great a cloud of witnesses ...."*

The "God is a consuming fire" part comes near the end of the sermon as the preacher offers a riff on the holiness of God. It's a complex few paragraphs contrasting the experience of God at Mt. Sinai and the promised experience of God at Mt. Zion, the heavenly city. The preacher is really bringing it now, complete with warnings of judgment and a reference to the sprinkled blood of Jesus, and the power of God shaking both the heavens and the earth. God at work shaking, purifying, sanctifying, hallowing. When you imagine with your ears, hearing the preacher of Hebrews, here at the end of the sermon you can hear how the preaching is finishing with some heat now. The preacher has set the table with "*Let us run with perseverance the race that is set before us,*" and "*Therefore lift your drooping hands and strengthen your weak knees,*" and "*Pursue peace with everyone,*" and "*See to it that no one fails to obtain the grace of God.*" The preacher has set the table and is bringing it home with more than a bit of hellfire and brimstone; bringing it home with the holiness of God. "*Since we are receiving a kingdom that cannot be shaken, let us give thanks by which we offer to God an acceptable worship with reverence and awe; for indeed, our God is a consuming fire.*"

A consuming fire that still judges, purifies, sanctifies, hallows, "holy-fies." A consuming fire that sparks in us, brings out of us, evokes in and from us the worship of our lives. A consuming fire that brings about, results in, forges a kingdom that cannot be shaken. A consuming fire. The action-oriented holiness of God. Don't ever stop it, God!

The "*hallowed be Thy name*" part is so easy to skip over and smoosh together with "*Our Father.*" But some days, probably most days, you and I and the world we live in could all use a bit more, call on a bit more, believe in a bit more, beg for a bit more of the action-oriented holiness of God. Living in response to the Gospel of Jesus Christ; it is a daily encounter. Right? Remembering your Baptism. Basking in God's grace, new every morning. Forgiveness afresh. But it's also the experience of growing in faith, and having rough edges softened, and yearning to be a better disciple. Your prayers at the end of the day, it's not just asking for forgiveness, it's asking God to help you be more faithful tomorrow. Keep being holy in my life, O God. Keep that fire burning.

Calling on, calling out the holiness of God. How else can you pray for the world today? How else could you have any hope for the world today? Our prayers of intercession, our prayers for peace, our prayers for the world, they presuppose and depend on the conviction that God is still at work; judging, purifying, sanctifying; that God is still at work bringing about justice and righteousness and peace; that God is still in it and at it. That the God of Abraham and Sarah, the God of our forebearers, the God we know in and through Jesus Christ, that with mystery and power and spirit, God was, and is, and ever shall be holy, that God is still holy. That God is working God's holiness; keeping God's name holy, and bringing about, working on, ushering in a kingdom that cannot be shaken. Don't stop now, God!

This holiness of God, this ongoing, ever-working holiness of God, it evokes in us, elicits from us, yes demands of us, our worship. The very worship of our lives. Our sacrifice of praise and thanksgiving is what we say when we are at the Table. God is holy and there is no other. If you're going to pray the Lord's Prayer on Tuesday, then you better be finding a place to sing on Sunday, because God is holy. I spent a few days in a meeting with Presbyterians from around the country this week. As always, there is the hand-wringing and worry about the state of the church and its future. But when you stop and think about it, God's people will always have a future in praise and worship, because God is holy. Here among God's people, the worship of the people of God—before you are here to be nurtured and fed by the Word, by God's promise, before you are here for the fellowship and companionship of God's people, before you are here to receive a blessing or experience the Spirit, or feast on some peace—before all of that, you are here because God is holy. God is evoking, eliciting, pulling out from within your praise, your thanksgiving, your worship. Keep it up, God! Keep on being holy!

You heard how I imagine the preacher from Hebrews bringing the heat and finishing the sermon; *our God is a consuming fire!* What if we gave our prayers, specifically the Lord's Prayer, a little "umph" when we pray the words? Rather than rushing by it, losing it in a rush to get to "*Thy kingdom come, Thy will be done,*" consciously slow down, and give it a little rhetorical, oratorical flare that is more fitting as a plea for the ongoing holiness of God and begs each day for the persistent, action-oriented holiness of God. Tonight, tomorrow, next week….

"Our Father, who art in heaven, *hallowed be Thy name!*"

He put before them another parable: "The kingdom of heaven is like a mustard seed that someone took and sowed in his field; it is the smallest of all the seeds, but when it has grown it is the greatest of shrubs and becomes a tree, so that the birds of the air come and make nests in its branches."

He told them another parable: "The kingdom of heaven is like yeast that a woman took and mixed in with three measures of flour until all of it was leavened."

The kingdom of heaven is like a mustard seed and a bit of leaven, like the greatest of shrubs and three measures of flour all leavened. *"The greatest of shrubs,"* Jesus said. Bible translations try different words to capture the intended image, the twist, even the humor. The greatest of shrubs. The greatest among herbs. The largest of garden plants. The largest of all vegetable plants. The greatest of shrubs. Sort of an oxymoron. Not like the Old Testament: Oaks of righteousness and mighty cedars of Lebanon. *"The greatest of shrubs,"* Jesus said.

In the high school yearbook when the senior class votes on "Most Likely to Succeed," "Best Athlete," and "King and Queen of the Prom," "Most Likely to Own Her Own Bio-tech

Company," "Most Likely to Become President Someday," or being voted "Best Date to Take Home to Mom or Dad," that's like being called the greatest of shrubs. The dreaded "back-handed compliment." The kingdom, as Jesus said, looks pretty good....for an herb. When it has grown, it is the greatest of shrubs and becomes a tree so that the birds of the air come and make nests in its branches.

The kingdom nests in the most unexpected places, and in the most unassuming ways. The kingdom of heaven doesn't soar from the pinnacles of power. It doesn't ride on the coattails of wealth. It isn't launched from the hallowed halls of the smartest, or even birthed in the practice of the most religious. The kingdom takes root and multiplies among the least, and the last, and the outcast, and the weak. Unnamed and unheralded, kingdom-bearers forward grace and make servanthood contagious while giving glory to God with the overwhelming ordinariness of their lives. Bearing witness allows the kingdom to stretch, whether they know it or not, offers a forearm shiver for the kingdom straight into the world's solar plexus where wealth and power, and self-interest and success, and violence and hatred all swirl with a life of their own. The kingdom of heaven is like the greatest of shrubs, and all of the leavened.

Years and years ago, my wife and I were given some Friendship Bread. Someone gives you some batter, some pre-dough, whatever you call it. It takes about ten days. You stir one day. You add something another day, then you split it all up, give some to friends, and bake your own loaf. We were newly married, and so we took the friendship project very seriously. It all went as smoothly as could be expected. We baked a loaf that was pretty good. Three

containers of stuff were ready to pass on to friends signi-
fying passing friendship forward. We delivered two of the
three right away. One bowl of batter, stored in a plastic
container, was left on the counter with the lid on to be
delivered the following morning. What happened over-
night could have made one of those old science fiction
movies. The next morning, the Friendship Bread batter
was everywhere. It was there on the counter, right above
the dishwasher that was run at bedtime and had heated
the countertop. The warmed batter pushed the lid off
the container and set out to take over the kitchen. It ran
off the counter, into the sink, and down the front of the
dishwasher. The batter was creeping everywhere. Even
the dog was frightened. That batter, the beginnings of
bread dough and the start of a loaf, were *all leavened* as
the scriptures said.

Kingdom creep. The constant presence and movement
of the kingdom of heaven, here and now. The kingdom
moving, here and now, and rarely with leaps and bounds.
Never with enough flow from the mountaintops of life.
Kingdom creep. Once in a while like a march for justice
across a bridge. More often with baby steps, one life, one
relationship, one voice at a time. And at times, far too easy
to look around and think that kingdom might be in retreat,
or the kingdom was closer back in the day, or the kingdom
thrived at the time of Jesus, or the kingdom peaked that
night in Bethlehem or that afternoon at Golgotha, or that
morning at the tomb. But Jesus taught that the kingdom
is on the move, until all of it, all of us, all of this, until all
of it is leavened. God at work. Ever-present, ever-moving,
with a subtle power that has the potential to knock the
lid off this world. The kingdom in our midst, creeping
into people's lives and reaching the world's darkest cor-

ners, offering a life of forgiveness and love, resurrection hope and joy, and a future unbound by fear. All of it in the name of, and through the work of, the One who said that the kingdom of heaven is like a mustard seed and a bit of leaven.

Just a few weeks ago, I was sitting with some clergy friends in a hotel lobby after a day's worth of meetings that ended with dinner. You're not going to believe me when I tell you this, but we were sitting there talking about particular verses, particular translations of the New Revised Standard Version of the Bible, that we find less than satisfying. That's a rip-roaring time, right? The only good news there is that, more often, when pastors get together they tell funeral stories or just talk about you church folks. So one of my colleagues lamented the lack of poetic license in the NRSV, and the perceived rigid commitment to the Greek text. The example was given of Jesus' first words spoken in the Gospel of Mark. Jesus said, *"The time is fulfilled, and the kingdom of God has come near; repent and believe in the good news."* That's the NRSV. The argument continued that in both the King James and in the Revised Standard versions, Jesus says, "the kingdom of God is at hand." Yes, the "come near" is closer to the actual Greek, but what the heck does that mean "come near," my friend pleaded with us. "Don't we believe the kingdom in and through Christ is something that can be touched, 'is at hand,' something that makes a difference all around us, all around here?" There was certainly some preaching going on. Don't knock sitting around a lobby bar talking Bible translation until you've tried it! *"The kingdom of God is at hand,"* Jesus said, "and it is like a mustard seed and a bit of leaven."

When Jesus instructs you to pray, *"Thy kingdom come, Thy will be done, on earth as it is in heaven,"* it's not a casual choice of words. The words come with quite a bit of baggage. The petition itself bears the weight of all the Lord's teaching on the kingdom of God. Jesus said a whole lot more about the kingdom than he ever said about the church. And you know, Jesus practiced what he taught; he prayed what he taught. In the Garden of Gethsemane, that night of his betrayal and arrest, that night of the Last Supper, the night before he was tortured and killed, Jesus prayed, *"Father, if you are willing, take this cup from me. Yet, not my will but yours be done."* Pray then like this, Jesus said. Pray then like I will, pray then like I do. *"Thy kingdom come, Thy will be done, on earth as it is in heaven."* The kingdom. God's Will. Pray it!

On earth as it is in heaven; in heaven where, as John Calvin puts it, "nothing is done apart from God's good pleasure." *As it is in heaven,* because there is no will in heaven other than yours, O God. No other will, no other forces, no one else at work in heaven but God. The connotation of the reference *"as it is in heaven"* is not for the heavenly city to suddenly appear, not for paradise to break out, not even for justice and righteousness to blossom in an end-time kind of way that wraps this life up with a bow and calls it a day. No, the plea is for God's will to unfold unabated, unfettered by the powers and principalities of the world, unencumbered by the world's present darkness. It is the cry for God's will to be at work in the world with a slow and steady kingdom creep to it all. The petition is for God's will to be freed in your life, in mine, God's will freed even from our own selves, our own voice, and our own will.

The prayer could not be any further from a social media frenzied world, where every voice and opinion is supposed to count. It could not be any more counter-cultural in a day when everyone demands a place at the table, nor could they be any more disconcerting in a consumer-driven religious marketplace that sells a whole lot of do it yourself, DIY spirituality. The traditional prayer makes a counter-intuitive move; it's not a centering prayer at all, as Dietrich Bonhoeffer would argue is because Christ is the center. It's a self-emptying prayer rather than a self-fulfilling one. So simple, yet so radical and so easy to miss. The radically God-centered nature of the Lord's Prayer. Just like in heaven where absolutely everything surrounds the throne of God's grace, and the One who sits upon the throne, the very Lamb of God, is in the midst of them all, in the center of it all. There where God wipes away every tear from their eyes.

When writing about prayer, the theologian Karl Barth describes it as an essential part of the Christian attitude. By Christian attitude, Barth seems to be describing the qualities, the character traits, the necessary ingredients of the Christian life. It's sort of interesting to add a contemporary overlay of the usage of the term "attitude." As in "he's got quite an attitude," or "you're going need a better attitude," or "she should lose the attitude," or "what's with the 'tude, dude?" Attitude these days seems to imply an edginess or a bit of moxie, unabashed, unfiltered assertiveness. This isn't actually too far from the important role that is the essence of prayer, according to Barth. For the Christian, before prayer is worship, before it is confession, before it is adoration, prayer, according to Karl Barth, it is unadulterated, honest, authentic petition. Or as he puts it, prayer is simply asking. As in "just asking." *Thy kingdom come, Thy will be done, on earth as it is in heaven.* I'm just asking, Lord. Just asking. The countercultural, counterintuitive, radical, subversive, not at all passive or naively pious petition of the Lord's Prayer. *Thy kingdom come, Thy will be done, on earth as it is in heaven.* Not so much of a complaint or lament as it is a petition with a bit of attitude. An affirmation, a belief, a conviction about the kingdom of heaven. It is so like a mustard seed and a bit of leaven.

Just last night, I sat over there listening to the combined choir from Nassau and Trinity sing the *Durufle Requiem*. It was beautiful. As the choir was singing, all these faces started snapping past as I closed my eyes. It was sort of like one of those award shows where someone sings and the pictures of those who had died in the last year flash on the screen. I was listening to the Requiem and found myself freshly surrounded by so great a cloud of witnesses. Thinking about this sermon, I sat there pondering how they shared, taught, witnessed and brought the kingdom to me. They were unheralded kingdom-bearers who forwarded grace and made servanthood contagious, and gave glory to God with the overwhelming ordinariness of their lives.

One of the faces I saw in my evening prayer was Sam Moffett's. I'm not sure I could name anyone in my life, in my cloud of witnesses, who had a greater impact on the spread of Christianity in the world, a greater impact on the kingdom than Dr. Moffett because of his ministry in Korea, and his impact on generations of servants sent out to the mission field. But Dr. Moffett's kingdom-sharing with me is going to sound so ordinary. Wherever I would see Dr. Moffet—on Sundays at the church door, back at coffee hour, or over at the retirement community—he would always say to me, "power to you." If you knew Dr. Moffett, then you knew what power he was talking about. For all I know, Sam Moffett said "power to you" to the mail carrier, the hostess at dinner, and every friend he ever had. But for me, what I heard, what I experienced every time he said it, was his prayer for me as pastor and proclaimer of the Gospel of Jesus Christ, that I would be lifted by the very power of God in service to God's kingdom. That God would bless me to share in a bit of kingdom creep. With all those faces flashing on the screen in my heart and soul last night, I found my shoulders lifting and I was sitting a bit taller, reminded of the kingdom work to which we have all been called. An affirmation, a belief, a conviction about the kingdom of heaven. Therefore, since you are surrounded by so great a cloud of witnesses, pray then like this…

"Thy kingdom come, Thy will be done, on earth as it is in heaven."

"Give Us This Day Our Daily Bread"

Matthew 14:13-21
LENT IV

Now when Jesus heard this, he withdrew from there in a boat to a deserted place by himself. But when the crowds heard it, they followed him on foot from the towns. When he went ashore, he saw a great crowd; and he had compassion for them and cured their sick. When it was evening, the disciples came to him and said, "This is a deserted place, and the hour is now late; send the crowds away so that they may go into the villages and buy food for themselves." Jesus said to them, "They need not go away; you give them something to eat." They replied, "We have nothing here but five loaves and two fish." And he said, "Bring them here to me." Then he ordered the crowds to sit down on the grass. Taking the five loaves and the two fish, he looked up to heaven, and blessed and broke the loaves, and gave them to the disciples, and the disciples gave them to the crowds. And all ate and were filled; and they took up what was left over of the broken pieces, twelve baskets full. And those who ate were about five thousand men, besides women and children.

The feeding of the five thousand. The multiplication of the loaves and fishes. It is the only miracle recorded in all four Gospels. It is difficult to imagine any story in the life of Jesus more familiar to the hearers of the Word, the readers of scripture. So it makes good sense to pair it with our petition for the day, *"Give us this day our daily bread."* It makes sense, when you pray that part of the Lord's Prayer, that the miracle scene of the loaves and fishes might flit across the screen of your imagination. It's so familiar, that story. Everyone must have some idea about what it must have looked like.

But I wonder what it sounded like? Dinner with five thousand people, plus women and children. I never thought about what it sounded like, until one morning when I was sitting in a Communion service at a beautiful spot next to the Sea of Galilee on a pastors' trip to the Holy Land. A breeze was blowing off the lake, and we were in the shade. The Table was set. We enjoyed some singing, but then, as we started to share the meal everything became amazingly quiet. We were coming forward two at a time to receive the bread and the wine. All of us in prayer. Some with tears. Others in wonder. It was a stunningly beautiful scene, not very far at all from where Jesus fed the five thousand.

We were still "communing" when three school buses pulled up just at the top of the hill. The children rushed out and made a beeline for the shore; they passed right in front of our view of the water and came right through our holy moment, our holy space. They weren't really much interested in the ancient church that was next door, the Church of the Primacy of St. Peter. They went straight for the water. Skipping stones, throwing rocks. In up to their knees. Laughing. Screaming. Yelling in Arabic. It's what children do along the shore. Not long after the children arrived, one of my fellow ministers, fearing the moment was going to be lost, stepped out from our gathering to try to appeal for quiet. He couldn't speak Arabic, so all he could do was "Shh!" as the kids ran all over. It was rather fruitless, if not downright funny to watch. The person next to me leaned over. "You know," he said, nodding toward the kids at the water's edge, "That's what this meal ought to sound like. That's what it is going to sound like in the kingdom of God."

Think what it must have sounded like with five thousand men, plus women and children, there by the Sea of Galilee. Jesus saw the "great crowd" and, according to the Gospel, *"He had compassion for them and cured their sick."* At the end of the day, the disciples had enough. It was late. Everyone was tired. People needed the time to go find some food. The disciples thought it would be best if "everyone was on their own for dinner." But Jesus said, *"They need not go away; you give them something to eat."* The disciples looked around at each other, at the crowd, at the food supply. They did the math and knew that five plus two would never equal five thousand adequately fed, not to mention women and children.

"Bring them here to me," Jesus said. One always assumes he's talking about the fish and bread: *"Bring them here to me."* Maybe he meant the people; the crowds; the men, women, and children. Those for whom he had such compassion. The sick. The hungry. The tired. *"Bring them here to me,"* Jesus said. Jesus told the crowds to sit down on the grass and, taking the five loaves and the two fish, he looked up to heaven, and blessed and broke the loaves, and gave them to his disciples, and the disciples gave them to the crowds. And everybody ate and was filled. They collected all the leftovers, twelve baskets full. A basket for each disciple. A basketful. Twelve. A perfect biblical number. A symbolic number, like infinity or *Pi* or something. The amount of leftovers. It was perfect. Just

right. Neverending. Those who ate were about five thousand men, besides women and children. Just think of what it all sounded like, that meal. Solitude, peace, and quiet. No way.

"Give us this day our daily bread." Maybe it is the one part of the prayer that ought not to come with solitude, peace, and quiet. It's the part of the prayer that comes with some rustling. The part of the prayer where you can hear movement. The part of the prayer that implies action. The part of the prayer that requires a partnership between God and God's people.

Every now and then we celebrate Communion by coming forward to receive the elements. When we do that here in the sanctuary or over in the chapel, after the meal and before I offer the concluding prayer, I often ask if everyone has been fed. It is not just a rhetorical question. It isn't quite like that outdated, no-longer-used inquiry at a marriage service, "Does anyone here know of any reason why this couple should not be joined in holy matrimony?" Has everyone been fed? It's not quite like that, I was asking to see if anyone had not received the elements, maybe someone who wasn't able to come forward, or a musician otherwise attending to worship. It is a question of hospitality, of liturgical etiquette.

Another pastor was leading a congregation in another church on another Lord's Day, in another celebration of the Lord's Supper. There were maybe forty or fifty folks gathered in the sanctuary and spread around the room like pepper on a dinner plate. It was a warm summer morning, so all the windows were open and the front doors, too. The men had even taken off their suit coats.

People could look out on farmland and country roads, and the homes dotted all around. This particular morning, all the sights and the sounds and the smells of the world were breaking in on the Communion celebration. Near the end of the service, after the elders had returned all the trays and everyone had been served, the pastor started to replace the fancy silver tops on the pile of trays that held all the cups and the leftover bread. Just before the hymn started, the pastor stopped with tray in hand, and with a pause that everyone noticed, the pastor looked out the window for a long time, as if looking all around town, as if pondering the dry summer that was hurting all the farmers, as if looking for the children spread all over the county. With an awkward pause, the pastor kept looking out the window, looking out at a congregation somehow differently defined. And then the pastor said, still looking out, "Has everyone been fed?"

It is a lot more than etiquette going when the church gathers at this Table. More than etiquette at the Lord's Table. A lot more than etiquette when it comes to the Lord's sacramental action. *Take. Bless. Break. Give.* It comes with an unwavering ethic about feeding the poor and caring for the sick and having compassion for those who suffer. *"Bring them here to me,"* Jesus said. And he took, and he blessed, and he broke, and he gave, and he fed them.

"Give us this day our daily bread." It ought to be so much more than your own sacramental yearning for the presence of Christ. When Jesus taught us to pray, it comes with an unwavering ethic about feeding the poor, caring for the sick, and having compassion for those who suffer!

I remember reading a blogging debate between a conservative evangelical pastor and a progressive liberal chaplain. Their conversation was posted on Belief.net. They were discussing whether it was more important for the church, or for a Christian, to offer spiritual sustenance or physical comfort to those who are suffering. If you had three hours to give on a Saturday morning, would you talk to people about salvation through Jesus, or would you serve at the soup kitchen? Should the church be saving souls or feeding the poor; or in the language of the prophet Isaiah, should God's people bring good news to the poor or bind up the brokenhearted. It wasn't much of a debate really because both faith leaders agreed that the answer was "Yes." Or as one of them concluded, "Jesus is the sandwich, and the sandwich is Jesus."

For those of us who follow Jesus, for those who were taught to pray by Jesus, the petition *"Give us this day our daily bread"* is more than a personal request for spiritual food sufficient for the day. Some parts of the prayer really need to be read with your eyes wide open. You can't look within without having first looked around.

Has everyone been fed?

Youth Sunday Sermon | ALEX MARTIN

Before Jesus fed five thousand hungry souls with only five loaves of bread and two fish, "he saw a great throng, and he had compassion on them, because they were like sheep without a shepherd; and he began to teach them many things" (Mark 6:34). Now, we've all seen Jesus and the idea of compassion thrown together in the same speech, just like we've seen Jesus teaching us valuable life lessons, leading by example. However, when we echo the Lord's Prayer, be it in our bed, at the dinner table, or on a Sunday morning, we solemnly ask the Lord to "*give us this day our daily bread.*" We don't know in what size, shape, or form this "daily bread" will be bestowed upon us, nor do we know the person, place, or circumstance from which it will be given. The whereabouts of it remain a mystery, while our yearning for that daily bread often feels insatiable.

When I first told my friend the story of Jesus feeding the five thousand, he said to me, "Man, those must have been some pretty small pieces of bread. How does that even come close to satisfying someone so hungry?" That question still sticks with me today as I ponder the significance of Jesus feeding the five thousand.

I'm going to share with you a story that appeared last summer on a local Tampa Bay news channel: Cherie Miller didn't even have to get out of her car to start something powerful. "I had my fingers on the wheel. I felt a sneaky, sly, happy feeling," Miller said. She stopped by the Chick-fil-A drive-thru in Temple Terrace, where that night proceeds were going toward her church, and decided she wanted to pass the blessing on. "I wanted to pay for the person behind me," she said. That started a chain reaction of generosity. One-by-one, strangers paid it forward, 18 in a row. "It was a way for me to pass on the love of God, and to give someone a surprise," she said. At the time, she had no idea of the ripple effect she started, but later when she returned for another order, she heard the good news and did it again. That time 20 people followed suit.[1]

For a few seconds, I would ask you all to close your eyes and just imagine what I am about to tell you: Imagine a tender, warm, baguette (preferably from the Witherspoon Bakery)... Now, try and divide that baguette into five thousand microscopic pieces. This may be tough to do, but now imagine *millions* of baguettes just falling from the sky, like the Witherspoon Bakery just decided to have a fire sale. Ok. You can open your eyes. For most of us, one five-thousandth of a piece of bread is barely anything. But, we have to realize, that to those who were fed, they were satisfied. Not because of the quantity of bread, but because of the action of giving. When we ask the Lord to *"Give us this day our daily bread,"* it can be hard to think that *we* are the ones who are to be sharing God's love and doing that giving (emptying our stock of bread is one idealistic example, I bet). But by imbuing such love and kindness into the world, we create what some call "a contagion of kindness." The story of Cherie Miller is such

1   Cascio, Josh. "Good Deed Sparks Chain Reaction at Local Chick-Fil-A." *My Fox Tampa Bay*. June 6, 2015. http://www.myfoxtampabay.com/story/25710194/good-deed-sparks-chain-reaction-at-local-chick-fil-a.

an example. With just one good deed, she led by example and 18 people gave each other what I would call "daily chicken." The next time she did it, two more people joined what she started.

Sometimes, however, the act of giving and receiving such daily bread is less overt. It's not every day that it will start raining baguettes. It doesn't involve paper bags and surely doesn't have someone literally "paying it forward" in random acts of kindness. Sometimes the daily bread is a compliment to that awkward girl you see everyone making fun of in the hallways on the way to class. Sometimes it's a sandwich for your contractor after he has bloodied his hands installing your new bathroom. Sometimes it's a smile to the teacher who labors tirelessly without a contract in front of caffeine-less students. Sometimes it's a tip to the single-mom waitress of 30% and not 20%.

I said earlier that when Jesus found the starving people they were like sheep without a shepherd. By asking the Lord to *"Give us this day our daily bread,"* we ask the Lord to help us be shepherds and to give the same compassion for others that Jesus had for us.

Youth Sunday Sermon | LILY OLSEN

Before the feeding of the five thousand, Jesus received the news of the death of John the Baptist. As anyone who had just received the news of the death of a cousin, or anyone close, he wanted to pray and take some time alone. Jesus went out on a boat to talk to God and hoped to end up in a deserted area. Before he made it there, the land filled with thousands of people. Instead of ending up in a deserted place, he found thousands of people waiting for him. Jesus felt compassion toward them and went to help. Although the small amount of time Jesus had in talking to God was probably not as long as he had hoped, he went out to help the people who needed his help. He performed the miracle of feeding five thousand people. They started with five loaves of bread and two fish, but ended with twelve baskets full of food after everyone ate. Every one there must have felt God's love through the miracle. To me, God's love was represented in this miracle because we may think God only has this small amount for each person, but really God has enough for everyone—and some left over.

Jesus taught the disciples the Lord's Prayer that included the line *"Give us this day our daily bread."* During the feeding of the five thousand, Jesus gave bread. At the Last Supper, he broke bread for his disciples as a symbol of his Body. Not only did the dinner and bread fill the disciple's stomachs, but it also filled their hearts. Even after Jesus died, he was still with each and every one of them. They had a part of the Body of Christ within them. As followers of Jesus, they went out to spread God's love. This love is the daily bread that we all need in our everyday lives.

Our senior high youth group has been able to go to a youth conference in North Carolina for many years. It has been a place for me to go over the past four summers and receive the Bread of Christ. Not only did we take Communion, but this conference has acted as a refresher and cleanser to me. Just seeing one thousand high school students in the same place, and who all believe together, is a reminder that "God's love is real and is alive today."

Over the last four years, we have had many memorable times at this conference. As an incoming freshman, there were only three people who I really knew at the beginning of this trip, but by the end of the week, we were all friends and one big family. All of the Nassau youth became a group and entered the weekly talent show. We learned a dance routine to an old school song, putting in hard work but also having fun. The night of the talent show, while on stage, one of the guys' shirts became untucked while doing a back flip. Since part of our signed contract stated that no exposed stomachs were allowed, the lights and music were immediately turned off even though we were in the middle of our routine. After all the other groups performed and the talent show was officially over, the Nassau group went out to the lawn and we did our dance again. As luck would have it, our speakers died. But then, all the people who were watching us started singing together. This conference was the only place I've ever seen a whole group of guys sing a song from a "boy band." I think it's God's love showing. Everyone wanted us to finish our dance because we had worked to learn it, but more importantly it showed that they wanted us to succeed. All the people were there to support us; sing for us when we had no music; watch us when we had no stage. Whether they knew it or not, their actions fed us the daily bread.

In December, Nassau's youth goes on another retreat to New York. This past year, anytime the speaker would say "Amen" we would reply, "That's wassup!" Let's try it—AMEN.

[Congregation replies] "That's wassup!"

I've heard the members of our youth group now use that as an everyday greeting and response. While "Amen" is an acclamation of Jesus' love, it is short enough that it doesn't stand out when said in the halls of high school or in town. Even though it is small, it is a daily reminder of God's love, and because of that, it is daily bread. AMEN.

[Congregation replies] "That's wassup!"

I find it easier to share God's love when surrounded by all Christians, like North Carolina, New York or at church. Sharing and nurturing others when I'm in a beautiful place surrounded by very similarly-aged people is easy. But in our everyday lives, we don't see God's love 24/7. I know God calls us to feed others who are different— different in age, religion, or culture.

While it is easy to feed the people we know, we still need to share it with everyone. When feeding the five thousand, Jesus broke bread for all the people, no matter their differences. God doesn't want only the "good" people to be loved, or the people who we are most comfortable with, but instead he wants everyone to be loved. As seen in the miracle of feeding the five thousand, just as God gave Jesus enough bread to feed everyone and some left over, God has enough love to share with all of us, and, even more. Not only does *"Give us this day our daily bread"* mean we need food in our stomach, but additionally it means we need God's love in our everyday life. Jesus' disciples received bread at the Last Supper, but they also gave the bread during the feeding of the five thousand. The Bible tells us that we are each a disciple of God. We will receive from him, but we are called to share his love. AMEN.

[Congregation replies] "That's wassup!"

Youth Sunday Sermon | NIKHIL PULIMOOD

"Give us this day our daily bread." Maybe that's why I love bread. Plain (unprocessed) bread can go a long way for me. I even have this pre-race ritual of eating a loaf with nothing else except a glass of water so that it digests. A full, family-sized, loaf of freshly baked bread can serve as a great snack for me. But that's the physical stuff—the stuff God meant when he said that we couldn't survive by bread alone. Obviously, when we ask God to give us this day our daily bread we aren't just asking for a baguette, but something more. The bread we ask for is greater than any tangible gift we could seek. It's the Bread of Life, the Living Bread, the stuff that gives life to the world.

So where does that bread come from? We can rule out Panera, and God hasn't been raining down manna for a few years. The source of the bread is found in our very appeal: *"Give us this day our daily bread."* The profound-ness in Jesus' words is that they are directed to God but are a call to each of us. No matter the time or place, we can be called to be deliverers and distributers of God's Word. That's one of those things you accept when you decide to be a Christian. Jesus, God on earth, gave us the quintes-sential example of this call.

Following his beloved cousin's death, Jesus went away to be alone with his disciples. Unfortunately, *"many saw them going and recognized them, and they hurried there on foot from all the towns and arrived ahead of them.*" Fully Divine, Jesus Christ was also fully human in flesh and blood. The time we take to recover, recuperate, and rejuvenate is essential to what we are as living beings. Despite his desire to be left alone, despite his need to take time to strengthen his human body, Jesus *"had compassion for them, because they were like sheep without a shepherd; and he began to teach them many things.*" He delivered to them the Bread of Life, the living bread, the stuff that gives life to the world. Then, to top it all off he performed his greatest miracle, the only one recorded in all four Gospels, the big kahuna for these people who he sees as sisters and brothers in need. Our Savior taught us that love has no timeline; as Christians we are always on call, ready to deliver the Bread of Life.

This past week, a classmate of mine made a decision that has no doubt changed the course of his life. A kid, with whom I've played on a soccer team and run middle school cross-country, posted something on social media that was regarded as a threat. It led to a thorough police investigation, which resulted in him being taken into custody. He may not have been a close friend of mine, but at 18 years old, a kid I have known for eight years could be convicted of a crime he committed out of foolishness. Nearly forty years ago, a friend of this congregation was unjustly convicted of a murder, despite clear evidence absolving him. He served 38 years in prison, was released, and then put back in prison due to a legal mishap. From where does the bread come for those incarcerated among the largest prison population in the world? Where do the many other casualties of the criminal justice system seek for spiritual, mental, and physical sustenance? That's where the pronoun "us" steps in. The collective us, the children of God, sinners and saints. Jesus Christ asked us to pray in this way to offer up a voice for those who have been silenced to the one who has already heard the mute. The prayer is not so much a grocery list offered up to the Almighty but a petition, a collective affirmation, a unified pronouncement that as children of God we love our sisters and brothers in Christ and accept our roles as deliverers of the Bread of Life, the living bread, the stuff that gives life to the world given to us by God.

"Forgive"

Then Peter came and said to him, "Lord, if another member of the Church sins against me, how often should I forgive? As many as seven times?" Jesus said to him, "Not seven times, but, I tell you, seventy-seven times. For this reason the kingdom of heaven may be compared to a king who wished to settle accounts with his slaves. When he began the reckoning, one who owed him ten thousand talents was brought to him; and, as he could not pay, his lord ordered him to be sold, together with his wife and children and all his possessions, and payment to be made. So the slave fell on his knees before him, saying, 'Have patience with me, and I will pay you everything.' And out of pity for him, the lord of that slave released him and forgave him the debt. But that same slave, as he went out, came upon one of his fellow slaves who owed him a hundred denarii; and seizing him by the throat, he said, 'Pay what you owe.' Then his fellow slave fell down and pleaded with him, 'Have patience with me, and I will pay you.' But he refused; then he went and threw him into prison until he would pay the debt. When his fellow slaves saw what had happened, they were greatly distressed, and they went and reported to their lord all that had taken place. Then his lord summoned him and said to him, 'You wicked slave! I forgave you all that debt because you pleaded with me. Should you not have had mercy on your fellow slave, as I had mercy on you?' And in anger

his lord handed him over to be tortured until he would
pay his entire debt. So my heavenly Father will also do
to every one of you, if you do not forgive your brother
or sister from your heart."

The 18th chapter of the Gospel of Matthew is full of the teachings of Jesus. No healings. No exorcisms. No conversations. No taking, breaking, and blessing of bread. Just teaching. Jesus teaching, and two brief questions from the disciples. Before the text we read just now, right at the beginning of chapter 18, the disciples asked Jesus, "Who is the greatest in the kingdom of heaven?" And then that question from Peter, "Lord, how often should I forgive." All the rest, here in Matthew 18, all the rest is from Jesus. It's all Jesus.

He calls a child over and puts the young one there among the disciples, *"Truly I tell you, unless you change and become like children you will never enter the kingdom of heaven." "Whoever welcomes one such child in my name welcomes me,"* he says. Jesus goes on to warn about putting a stumbling block before a little one, and he does one of those rhetorical hyperbolic riffs about cutting off body parts and tearing out eyes that can cause you to stumble. And he tells that one about the shepherd who has a hundred sheep and leaves the ninety-nine to go in search of the one that went astray. *"I tell you, he rejoices over it more than the ninety-nine that never went astray. It is not the will of your Father in heaven that one of these little ones should be lost,"* Jesus says.

But he's not done! Here, still in the same chapter, Jesus offers that teaching about taking one or two of the members with you to visit a brother or sister who has sinned against you. It's a rather detailed process that he gives. *"If the member refuses to listen to them, tell it to the church."* If the offender still refuses, let them be like a tax collector to you. *"Truly I tell you, whatever you bind on earth will be bound in heaven, and whatever you loose on earth will be loosed in heaven."* If two or three of you agree on anything you ask, Jesus says, it will be done. *"For where two or three are gathered in my name, I am there among them."* There's that priceless promise about the presence of Christ forever sealed into the church's collective soul. It comes not in a vignette about the disciples at worship or an exhortation about them doing mighty things with just small numbers, it comes in Jesus' teaching about discipline, accountability, and forgiveness.

"Then Peter came and said to Jesus, 'Lord if a brother or sister sins against me, how often should I forgive? As many as seven times?' Jesus said to him, 'Not seven times, but I tell you, seventy times seven times.'" Which, in terms of biblical numbers, any way you shape it, Jesus is telling Peter that you have to do it this many times (fingers flashing). Put another way, you have to do it every time, forgive *every time*. *"For this reason,"* Jesus says, *"the kingdom of heaven may be compared to...."*

Here, in this chapter, that's pretty much all from the lips of Jesus. After Peter asks about how many times he needs to forgive, Jesus doesn't look around the room to find someone to use as an object lesson on forgiveness so that Peter can practice. He doesn't lay out a step-by-step process on forgiveness that involves this member, and then these members, and then the church. He doesn't try to parse the word "forgiveness" in a Sermon on the Mount kind of way like he did with "adultery" (defining it as in the heart). He doesn't give a real life example, like when he taught on generosity by pointing to the poor widow who put in the two copper coins, which was all the living that she had. He doesn't get practical and specific, like when he tells the disciples to "pray then like this." No, when Peter asks Jesus how often he has to forgive someone, Jesus says that *"for this reason the kingdom of heaven may be compared to…."* And he goes on to tell them the parable about the king and the unforgiving servant.

A king decides its time to settle up with all the help. One slave has run up a debt so large it is beyond calculation. The text says "ten thousand talents." That's 150,000 year's worth of wages for a worker. The debt was a million-zillon-gazillion. After the king orders the man and his family to be sold and all their possessions liquidated in order to salvage a "million-zillion-gazillioneth" of a basis point on the debt return, the slave asks for patience and promises to pay back everything; this of course is insultingly impossible. The king, however, has pity on the slave, releases him. AND FORGIVES THE DEBT!

That same slave, that same day, or as the Bible might put it elsewhere, "immediately" that same slave went out and came upon a colleague, a fellow servant, another slave who owed him ten or twenty bucks. The freshly-forgiven slave grabs the other by the throat, demanding to be paid. "Give me a break. I will pay," was the response of the slave being choked, the one who couldn't breathe. The debt-free slave refuses and demands that the one who had borrowed something like a day's wage be thrown into prison until he pays, which of course he would not be able to do from prison with any earnable income now off the table. Some other slaves captured the whole thing on their cell phones and went and showed the video to the king, who was so mad at the wicked slave's unwillingness to pass "debt forgiveness" forward that he handed him over to be tortured until he would pay his entire debt of a million, zillion, gazillion, which means he was to be tortured forever. *"So my heavenly Father will also do to everyone of one of you, if you do not forgive your brother or your sister from your heart,"* Jesus offers the editorial exclamation point to the parable. And Peter looks at the other disciples, and asks in somewhat of a whisper, "The Word of the Lord?"

All the ways and the things Jesus taught in Matthew 18, all that form and content about being humble like a child and not being a stumbling block, and searching for the one lost, and taking members with you to confront someone who has wronged you, after all of that, when it comes to forgiveness, Jesus tells this blasted parable. It was like Jesus somehow knew that humankind forever would have a much more visceral reaction and have a harder time forgiving debt than forgiving sin. It's interesting how many commentators, preachers, and teachers point to Jesus' use of humor here. Humor, I guess, in the hyperbole of the size of the debt. But as the saints in my first congregation would say, "It might be funny, but it's not 'ha-ha.' There are many other adjectives one could use to describe the parable before getting to "funny." Chilling. Disconcerting. Violent. Assertive. Absurd. Upsetting. Sure, the debt is a crazy amount, but what about the "seizing around the neck and the thrown in jail for 20 bucks and the tortured" part. The only other reference to torture in the four gospels is the suffering of Jesus.

Oh, and then Jesus comments on the parable, mentioning that the heavenly Father will do that to you also if you do not forgive. Jesus is wickedly serious about forgiveness! You don't explain away a parable like this. You certainly don't chuckle it away, either. All you can do is let it knock you off kilter, make your head spin, and jerk the chain of your heart over and over again. Because God's forgiveness of us is absurd, and God's call for us to forgive is chillingly assertive.

Forgive us our debts as we forgive our debtors. Forgive us our trespasses as we forgive those who trespass against us. Forgive us our sin as we forgive those who sin against us. Debts. Trespassses. Sins. Translation confusion abounds. As Carol Wehrheim notes, "Perhaps the best thing to do is to focus on the verb in the prayer: forgive." When it comes to forgiveness, Jesus isn't messing around. While you and I are trying to figure out which is the best word to use, what works best with children, what makes sense up here (in the brain), what offers the better connotation and reflects our Lord's intent (sins, trespasses, debts), Jesus is off telling the parable about the king and the unforgiving servant. While you and I are still talking about how difficult forgiveness can be, and whether or not one can or has to forgive and forget, Jesus has already moved on to tell the parable about the king and the unforgiving servant. While you and I are engaged in healthy and meaningful theological banter about whether forgiveness comes only after someone asks, or whether repentance is a prerequisite for forgiveness and necessary for justice to flow, Jesus is yet again telling the parable about the king and the unforgiving servant. While you and I are rightly regaling one another with stories of famous forgivers, like Nelson Mandela or Ernie Zamperini, Jesus tells the parable about the king and the unforgiving servant yet one more time. "Jesus, what does it mean, 'Forgive us our sins, as we forgive those who sin against us." Jesus responds, *"The kingdom of heaven may be compared to ... "*

It happens pretty regularly in an ecumenical gathering where the Lord's Prayer is said. Ecumenical gathering, not a meeting, but a wedding or a funeral or an occasional community worship service. The Lord's Prayer is said, and all the Methodists and the Roman Catholics, and the Episcopalians and the Baptists, and the Presbyterians all join in. There is that awkward moment in the cadence, right? It happened again yesterday at Margaret Merrill's memorial service. Those in the room who say debts and debtors, they have to wait, they have to pause, for the others to catch up; as we forgive those who trespass against us, who sin against us. Call it the debtors pause. What if the pause was more than just an act of hospitality and a good practice for successful unison prayer? What if everyone praying the Lord's Prayer, what if we all (trespasses, sins, debts), what if everyone just stopped at that point? There ought to be a pause, a break, a silence. Forgiveness: it's all so beyond words. And when you are confronted once again with the absurd forgiveness of God, and God's chillingly assertive expectation that you will forgive, it ought to knock you off kilter, make your head spin, and jerk the chain of your heart over and over again.

"Lead Us"

*Then Jesus was led up by the Spirit into the wilderness
to be tempted by the devil. He fasted for forty days
and forty nights, and afterwards he was famished.
The tempter came and said to him, "If you are the Son
of God, command these stones to become loaves of
bread." But he answered, "It is written, 'One does not
live by bread alone, but by every word that comes from
the mouth of God.'"*

*Then the devil took him to the holy city and placed him
on the pinnacle of the temple, saying to him, "If you are
the Son of God, throw yourself down; for it is written,
'He will command his angels concerning you,' and 'On
their hands they will bear you up, so that you will not
dash your foot against a stone.'"*

*Jesus said to him, "Again it is written, 'Do not put the
Lord your God to the test.'" Again, the devil took him to
a very high mountain and showed him all the king-
doms of the world and their splendour; and he said to
him, "All these I will give you, if you will fall down and
worship me." Jesus said to him, "Away with you, Satan!
For it is written, 'Worship the Lord your God, and serve
only him.'"*

*Then the devil left him, and suddenly angels came and
waited on him.*

Do not bring us to the time of trial, but rescue us from the evil one. Lead us not into temptation, but deliver us from evil. Save us from the time of trial and deliver us from evil. Trial. Temptation. Test. *"God is faithful, and God will not let you be tested beyond your strength, but with the testing God will also provide the way out so that you may be able to endure it."* That's I Corinthians 10. The Apostle Paul. Testing. Temptation Trial. I Peter 1: *"In this you rejoice, even if now for a little while you have had to suffer various trials, so that the genuineness of your faith—being more precious than gold that, though perishable, is tested by fire—may be found to result in praise and glory and honor when Jesus Christ is revealed."* The Book of James: *"Blessed is anyone who endures temptation. Such a one has stood the test and will receive the crown of life that the Lord has promised to those who love the Lord. No one, when tempted, should say 'I am being tempted by God,' for God cannot be tempted by evil and God tempts no one. But one is tempted by one's own desire, being lured and enticed by it."* Trial. Temptation. Testing. That night in the garden, when the disciples couldn't stay awake even though Jesus asked them to. Jesus said to them, *"Stay awake and pray that you may not come into the time of trial; the spirit is indeed willing but the flesh is weak."* The time of trial. The time of testing. The time of temptation.

This one petition in the Lord's Prayer is not a summary of the New Testament witness when it comes to trial and temptation. It is not a theological thesis statement on testing, faith, life, and the providence of God. It is a petition. A prayer. It is not a philosophical statement on the problem of evil. It's the teaching of Jesus on prayer. Pray, then, in this way: Do not bring us into temptation, but rescue us from evil.

Of course, Jesus had his own recorded, iconic experience of temptation, trial, and testing. It is in Matthew's telling of the Sermon on the Mount that we read of the Lord's Prayer. According to Matthew, Jesus was led up by the Spirit into the wilderness to be tempted by the devil. Scholars point out that the Lord's encounter with the devil here follows a familiar pattern with this order of the temptations: hunger, putting God to the test, false worship. It is the same pattern from the Hebrew Bible of Israel's wandering in the wilderness. The timeless wilderness connection is affirmed all the more by the response of Jesus, by his defense, and his quotes from Deuteronomy. As one commentator points out, those wilderness trials, before they were his, they were Israel's. Feeding yourself first. Putting God to the test. Creating and worshipping false gods. Before they were his, they were the trials of God's people. And after they were his, they are the trials of God's people. Jesus in the wilderness. It's a prototype of sorts. An example, with a capital "E," of the testing that comes in the world's wilderness. Not just this temptation or that temptation; one vice, another sin. No, it is a portrayal of how the principalities and powers of darkness tear away at the very core of what it means to be God's people, God's children. Jesus and his wilderness testing. It is the role model, the prototype, the archetype, the veritable definition of obedience and faithfulness for a child of God.

And on this Palm Sunday, we find ourselves, yet again, somewhere along the pathway as Jesus rides on. As he goes up to the city that was in turmoil. A city full of swirling chaos, where the forces of evil are out to destroy him and the kingdom that comes with him. The city where shouts of "Crucify him" will reduce any "hosanna" to a faint echo of yesterday. Turmoil. Chaos. The taunts. The mocking. The jeering that will surely come. *"If you are the Son of God, come down from the cross."* A wilderness taunt that Jesus has heard before. It's Palm Sunday, and Jesus is in full obedience, his faithfulnesss on display for all to see as he rides on. Jesus is heading into an urban wilderness to be tried, tested, tempted; tested by death itself. He still rides on... *"though he was in the form of God, he did not regard equality with God as something to be exploited, but emptied himself, taking the form of a slave, being born in human likeness. And being found in human form, he humbled himself and became obedient to the point of death—even death on the cross."* (Philippians)

Pray then like this, Jesus said, "Lead us not into temptation but deliver us from evil." This petition in the Lord's Prayer is about more than one temptation, one vice, this sin or that one. It's not the sound track for a morality play. Without question, prayer is essential when it comes to humankind battling the ways of the flesh. Anyone in a 12-step program will attest to the importance of prayer. Any parent, who watches their high school student pull out of the driveway on a Friday night, understands the necessity of prayer. A couple celebrating their 60th wedding anniversary will give witness to the effectiveness of prayer in their lifetime of fidelity and faithfulness to one another. A business person rises to offer gratitude for the role of prayer in their daily battle to put on the whole armor of God in the ongoing test between what's right and wrong. The prayer lives of God's people are full to overflowing with the plea of helping us in the battle against the way of all flesh. In the thick of one of those brutally honest conversations with God Almighty, a whole lot of other words, groans, and cries, and pleas, and shouts are going to be offered before you get to *"Save us from the time of trial and deliver us from evil."*

Every Sunday when we have Communion, the serving teams meet in my office. They get themselves organized, and look for a substitute or two, if necessary. When everything is ready, and the start of worship has drawn near, we pray together; as those elders and deacons are heading out of my office, I almost always say, "Be careful out there." It is a silly quote from an old television show, "Hill Street Blues." The commanding officer, after the morning briefing, would say, "Be careful out there" on every episode. It has been pointed out to me that the one morning I didn't say "Be careful out there" was the one time anyone can remember when we had a significant stumble and spill. It's a symbolic exhortation to Communion servers, and then to worshippers heading out, the people of God being sent into the world. "Hey, let's be careful out there."

The petition of the Lord's Prayer that includes trial, testing, temptation, and evil, is a "help us be careful" out there plea. This does not mean to just be careful in terms of sin, morality, and our good and bad choices, but to be careful in terms of obedience and faithfulness. Being mindful of who God in Jesus Christ has called us to be. Being reminded that powers and principalities are at work in very real ways, tearing away at your life and mine, tearing away at the core of what it means for us to be children of God. The petition is a weekly, daily, a few times a day plea to God that God will empower us, shape us, and lead us in service to the Gospel. You don't just stumble upon this language in the Lord's Prayer. It comes just paragraphs after Jesus' own wilderness testing. It comes firmly embedded in the Gospel narrative that follows him all the way to the cross. Pray then like this: that we who are so surrounded in the world's darkness, that we might somehow, someway reflect the light of his obedience and that everything that works against the kingdom of God here on earth might cower at the power of him who is at work in us.

This petition of the Lord's Prayer may get worked over more than all the others as translators, commentators, you, me and we all try to understand and find meaning. But through it all in this part of the prayer, and in the whole prayer for that matter, no one ever questions the plural part. Us. Our. We. Save us from the time of trial and deliver us from evil. It has a strikingly plain sense to it when you stop and ponder the plural. It's not about your trials, temptations, tests. It's about ours. The children of God. The Body of Christ. God's people. It's about our faithfulness and obedience amid the world's turmoil. God's own people amid the world's testing, the world's temptation, the world's trial. Marked at our Baptism. Nurtured at his Table. Claimed at the cross as God's own. God's people. *"You are God's own people, in order that you may proclaim the mighty acts of the one who called you out of darkness into God's marvelous light"* (I Peter).

To stand here along the way, watching him ride on, is to be drawn in once again to his complete obedience and his incomparable faithfulness. To watch him ride on is to be spellbound, once again, by his perfect love. To watch him ride on is to have the breadth of his life and teaching and action; it all passes before your eyes. His words, his healing touch, his broken heart, his own tears, his embrace of the sinner, his poke at the pious, his challenge to the rich, his abiding concern for the poor, the sick, the grieving. It's all right there as he rides on. To watch him ride on toward humanity's wilderness, with the cross being fashioned on the horizon, is to be reminded afresh of the powers and principalities of darkness that still work to destroy him and the kingdom that comes with him. To watch him ride on is to realize what's left along the way, all that's left as he rides on, is neither palms strewn along the way, nor cloaks tossed in the road. What's left after the parade has passed by, what's left is us. We're sort of all he has left. Us and the Holy Spirit (thank God). It's us. We're God's people.

Claimed, shaped, saved, sent yet again by his complete obedience, his incomparable faithfulness, and his perfect love. And as he rides out of sight, as it all starts to sink in, someone somewhere in the Body of Christ, calls after him, hoping that he can still hear as he is way up that hill.

Jesus! Hey Jesus, save us from the time of trial! Deliver us from evil! Hosanna!

"Forever"

After the Sabbath, as the first day of the week was dawning, Mary Magdalene and the other Mary went to see the tomb. And suddenly there was a great earthquake; for an angel of the Lord, descending from heaven, came and rolled back the stone and sat on it. His appearance was like lightning, and his clothing white as snow. For fear of him, the guards shook and became like dead men. But the angel said to the women, "Do not be afraid; I know that you are looking for Jesus, who was crucified. He is not here; for he has been raised, as he said. Come, see the place where he lay. Then go quickly and tell his disciples, 'He has been raised from the dead, and indeed he is going ahead of you to Galilee; there you will see him.' This is my message for you." So they left the tomb quickly with fear and great joy, and ran to tell his disciples. Suddenly Jesus met them and said, "Greetings!" And they came to him, took hold of his feet, and worshipped him. Then Jesus said to them, "Do not be afraid; go and tell my brothers to go to Galilee; there they will see me."

Fear and great joy, as in *"they left the tomb quickly with fear and great joy."* Fear and great joy. It is a jarring combination of emotions. It's not something to really be explained. You don't make sense of it. Fear and great joy. But the combination, it is part of the human experience. You can't explain it, but you've seen it. I've seen it. An 18-year-old arrives on a college campus somewhere, anywhere. She is so glad to be out of high school. She is, honestly, so happy to be away from home. But her chief goal that first week is to not let her roommates know how wicked scared she is. Fear and great joy. Ask any first-time parents who have just brought a baby home from the hospital, or who've just arrived home with their adopted newborn. Ask any first-time parents, and without using the exact words, I assure you they will describe both fear and great joy to you. When both dads take the morning off from work because their son is getting on the bus for the first time and heading off to first grade? That moment when the bus drives away is fear and great joy. The saint of the church, with a fullness of life far beyond what the psalmist describes, four score by reason of strength, that pillar of faith and strength who is both ready to go to glory and anxious about getting there. That's fear and great joy. You can't really describe it, but you've seen it. You've tasted it. You know it.

The only thing mentioned more than Jesus being raised in Matthew's account of the empty tomb is fear. For fear of the stone-rolling, stone-sitting, earthquake-announcing angel, those guards shook and became like dead men. To the women there at the now-empty tomb, the angel said, "Do not be afraid." Do not fear. When they left the tomb quickly, it was with fear and great joy. And then suddenly Jesus met them, and as they clung to his feet and fell down and worshipped him, he said, "Do not be afraid." Do not fear. Some translations, commentators, or preachers try to soften the fear, opting for the word "awe" or "wonder." They try to go with that old biblical use of the word "fear," as in "the fear of the Lord is the beginning of wisdom" (Psalm 111). Fear, as in worship and reverence. "Filled with awe and a lot of excitement," the women left the tomb quickly. No, they were scared to death, scared by death, sacred of the mystery that life might somehow rise out of death. Otherwise, the risen Jesus would not have said to them, "Do not be afraid." It was fear and great joy.

Not all that many weeks ago, I was over at Princeton Cemetery for the burial of ashes. It was one of those bitter cold, single digit kind of days. When I arrived at the cemetery, I was warned that the pathway back to the grave was long and treacherous because of ice and snow. It was a large, extended family gathering and they arrived in sort of shifts. So the first of us at the grave had to wait. Even though it was cold, it always seems colder in a cemetery. At one point we were waiting for the last carload to make their way down that pathway. They couldn't move fast, although they were trying. Did I mention that it was really cold? The older family members and I had been waiting out there for quite awhile by then. The liturgy at the grave was brief, but I made the pastoral call to be even more brief that frigid afternoon. After I gave the benediction, there amid the silence, a young great-grandchild spoke up loud enough for everyone to hear, "Don't we have to sing something?" An older voice around the circle said something like, "we can sing later." But the child was right, of course, about having to sing.

Not all that many days ago, again at Princeton Cemetery, as what would be the last snow flakes started to fall that Friday morning, we stood around the open grave. Snow now sticking to us, on the flowers, on the casket. I finished with the benediction and there amid the silence, a lone voice started to sing, "Amazing Grace." It was without cue, without plan. But we all joined in, even the funeral director standing behind me holding an umbrella over me was singing in my ear. "I once was lost, but now am found." There at the grave, as winter was offering a last gasp and death was demanding to be the exclamation point in life, the song was a daring act of praise. That lone voice that had started and led us, just as the great-grandchild weeks before, knew we had to sing. Surrounded by death, yet still bold enough to sing God's praises. It's what fear and great joy sound like. A daring, death-stomping doxology.

Doxology. Literally, "words of glory." An ascription of praise to God. Like "glory to God in the highest." Doxology. Like "praise God from whom all blessings flow." Doxology. An act of praise to God that often includes the word "glory." As in "for thine is the kingdom, and the power, and the glory, forever." The last line in the Lord's Prayer. It is doxology. A doxology appended to the prayer in the earliest days of the ancient church. For careful readers of Matthew's Gospel, it is a footnote referencing some early manuscripts. *"For Thine is the kingdom, the power, and the glory."* Forever confusing generations of the faithful, who wondered whether Protestants or Catholics had it right. Is it in? Is it out? Do we stop? Are we finished? What's the deal on the Lord's Prayer, pastor? Father? Nobody's right. Nobody's wrong. It's simply a bold offering of praise in the prayer life of some of the earliest Christians. John Calvin argued that no one would dare offer such prayer to God based on the worth, the merit, of the one doing the praying. The last line commends the prayer, lifts the prayer, frames the prayer in the justice and righteous-flowing kingdom, the death-conquering power, and the breathtaking glory of God—all of which is forever, and ever, and ever. Hallelujah, Hallelujah.

My high school football team huddled up before each half of every game, just like all teams in every sport. It wasn't "team on three," or a captain yelling "who are we" and the team shouting back in response. No, we took off our helmets, knelt down, and said the Lord's Prayer. My public high school. Before you applaud the coach's piety, let me describe how the prayer ended. The pace of the prayer quickened throughout, and by the time we came to "for Thine is the kingdom.." all of our voices were raised. Here's how it finished... "*For thine is kingdom, the power* ... (turns to a shout and scream)." Everyone rose to their feet, with shouts and cries... now including "Let's go out there and crush them!" It wasn't piety. It wasn't praise. It wasn't even prayer. It was a pre-game ritual, a sideline pep talk, something akin to a motivational speaker!

I have felt guilty about that Lord's Prayer abuse for 35 years, until this week. I finally found a lesson in it, a more meaningful take-away. No, that sideline experience will never be deemed holy. But how that last line, how the *"For Thine is the kingdom"* part turned to a shout, it reminds me of how doxology can become a shout of praise? Easter morning for the followers of Jesus is our shout of praise. Easter morning is when doxology becomes a shout. You and I gathered here, it is all praise, total praise, all doxology brought about, brought forth, caused by that empty tomb, and the stone-rolling angel, and the "he has been raised" part of the Gospel witness. Easter morning is for us to pray, *"For Thine is the kingdom, and the power, and the glory* (turns to shouts)." Christ is risen! He is risen, indeed! A daring, death-stomping doxological shout! It's what fear and great joy sound like.

Fear and great joy. You can't really describe it, but you've seen it. You've tasted it. You know it. The women at the tomb were scared to death, scared by death, scared by the mystery that life might somehow rise out of death. Scared to death. Been there. Scared by death. Check. Yes. But it's difficult to say what's so scary about the life rising out of death part. What's scary about resurrection? Is it the mystery of it all? Is it the 'after three days he rose just like he said' part? Is it that in rising from the dead he has forever transformed the power that sin and death can have over us? Is it how in coming out of the tomb he has promised eternal life to us and opened the way to new life now, abundant life now? Is that what's scary? Or is the scarier part the notion that you and I will never be able to wrap our minds around it? For most of us, probably, for most of us in a congregation like ours, in a town like this, where the (PhD) stripes rule and smarter is always better, that's the scary part, right? You'll never get it!

"Do not be afraid," Jesus said to them, "go and tell them to go to Galilee; there they will see me." Jesus sent them out to Galilee, that 'kingdom has come near' place, that place of kingdom talk and kingdom work....where the children and the widows, and imprisoned and the sick, and the dying are cared for...where sinners are welcomed and tax collectors are transformed, and the unclean are embraced... where parables are told and lived, the one about a father embracing a lost son, and the one about a foreigner helping the one in the ditch, and the one about how you can't serve God and mammon....where the Gospel is taught and lived: turning the other cheek, caring for the poor, loving your enemies, and forgiving over and over. The women and the disciples and us, the risen Jesus

sent them; he sends us out to do his work and says, "Yeah, I will see you there." Do not be afraid!

Easter morning has already come and gone in Kenya. It is a nation that has been so shaken by the brutal murders on a college campus of almost 150 mostly Christian people, killed for no other reason than for their answer of "I am a Christian." It is a faith-laden tragedy beyond what you and I can imagine. Here's what has been stirring in my heart this weekend. The followers of Jesus gathered all over Kenya earlier today. You know it. I know it. We don't have to wait to read about it, or see a story about it. It's Easter Day and those dear, dear Christian sisters and brothers gathered to weep and to pray and to, yes, to offer a daring, death-stomping doxology. And someone had to say it, had to start to sing it. Someone did. Surrounded by death, with nothing to cling to other than the resurrection power of God, and still bold enough to pray, *"For Thine is the kingdom, and the power, and the glory forever."* A defiant, doxological shout. You know they said it. And this morning, this Easter day, Christians all around the world say it with them. Because we have to. We have to because of him. Because....

Christ is risen! He is risen, indeed!

"It's a Hard Stop"

Mark 16:1-8

EASTER II

When the Sabbath was over, Mary Magdalene, and Mary the mother of James, and Salome bought spices, so that they might go and anoint him. And very early on the first day of the week, when the sun had risen, they went to the tomb. They had been saying to one another, "Who will roll away the stone for us from the entrance to the tomb?" When they looked up, they saw that the stone, which was very large, had already been rolled back. As they entered the tomb, they saw a young man, dressed in a white robe, sitting on the right side; and they were alarmed. But he said to them, "Do not be alarmed; you are looking for Jesus of Nazareth, who was crucified. He has been raised; he is not here. Look, there is the place they laid him. But go, tell his disciples and Peter that he is going ahead of you to Galilee; there you will see him, just as he told you." So they went out and fled from the tomb, for terror and amazement had seized them; and they said nothing to anyone, for they were afraid.

It's a hard place to stop. *"They said nothing to anyone, for they were afraid."* Mark's account of the empty tomb at the end of his Gospel. *"They said nothing to anyone, for they were afraid."* No greeting from the risen Jesus. No risen Jesus for that matter. Yes, the stone is rolled back. There is a young man dressed in white, who tells the

women that Jesus has been raised. He is not here. The
women, according to Mark, fled from the tomb in terror
and amazement. No "fear and great joy." Just fear. *"They
said nothing to anyone, for they were afraid."* It's a hard
place to stop.

When you read the 16th chapter of Mark, if you were
following along as I read the first 8 verses to you, you
will see all kinds of brackets and footnotes and margin
notes and paragraph headings. Bible editors and Bible
translators try to make the reader aware of the critical
work that has been done related to the ending of Mark's
Gospel. Ancient manuscripts lack consensus, and so one
finds a shorter ending and a longer ending and an ending-
ending. Beyond what the scholars write about, in terms of
historic sources and the Greek style of language, parts of
the second half of chapter 16 sort of don't pass the sniff test
(a highly technical term in biblical scholarship). Snake
handling and drinking deadly things but not getting hurt,
and the risen Jesus "upbraiding" the disciples for their
lack of faith and stubbornness, and Jesus sending out
through them "the sacred and imperishable proclamation
of eternal salvation." That phrase sounds less "Gospelly"
and much more like a sentence from a final paper over
at the seminary. The consensus among New Testament
scholars is that the ending-ending is here at v. 8. *"They
said nothing to anyone, for they were afraid."* Yes, it's a hard
place to stop, but it's a hard stop. Mark ends here.

I read the novel *Gone Girl* awhile back. When the movie
came out, I kept reading even though I heard moviegoers
complain that they didn't like the ending. When I finally
did see the movie, the ending of the movie was pretty
much exactly like the ending of the book. Some people

didn't like it, but the ending was the ending. When it comes to the Gospel of Mark, it would seem that folks didn't like the ending. The earliest scribes, church fathers in the first centuries and establishers of the canon didn't like the ending and, after all, who wants to stop at *"They said nothing to anyone, for they were afraid?"* So we're left with a shorter ending and a longer ending and an ending-ending. On a morning like last Sunday, it's not easy to stick with Mark and a hard stop at v. 8 when the sanctuary is full, the brass are playing, and everyone is waiting to sing "Thine is the Glory." Then the preacher announces that the first proclaimers of the Easter message fled in "silence and fear." Cue the trumpets!

Don Juel was a professor of New Testament at Princeton Seminary and a worshipping member of Nassau Church, along with his wife, Linda. Don died in 2003. Others can describe his legacy more fully than I can, but I can't imagine anyone wrote about the ending of Mark's Gospel in a more compelling, more provocative, more faithful way than Don Juel. The hard stop at v. 8, *"They said nothing to anyone, for they were afraid,"* for him, was no longer up for discussion. What's most captivating about Juel's work is how he sees good news in THIS ending, and how he sees the very promise of God in THIS ending to Mark.

With what must have been a bit of devilish humor, Don once preached a sermon on the longer ending of Mark; after reading Mark 16:9-19, he said to the gathered community, "I will confess that I have never heard those words....read in church. And I hope I never will again." Juel went on in that sermon, which was of course on the ending-ending and not the longer ending, he went on to say this: "People can't leave the ending alone: it's too unsettling. What terrified the women who went to the tomb, loaded down with spices to do their duty to the corpse, was that Jesus wasn't there... As the Gospel ends, Jesus isn't there. He is nowhere to be seen. There's not even a garment to touch."

"When you reach the end of the story," Professor Juel preached, "Jesus isn't there....It's a good thing. If we could get our hands on Jesus, we would surely throttle the life out of him, as did his contemporaries. But we can't. Jesus is free, out of the tomb, beyond our control, and beyond death. That's why the story is good news. He's free so that he can make his way into our lives and actually liberate as God had planned since before the foundation of the world." Here's the provocative trajectory of Juel's thought: If you are going try to keep the risen Jesus under your thumb, if you're going to forever link resurrection hope to a pious effort to cling to his feet or to hear him call your name, holding on to a conception of Jesus that simply confirms all your expectations and assumptions, if you're going to limit God's liberating promise to the requirements of your intellect, your imagination, or your satisfaction, if God's entire Easter enterprise results in little more than (in Juel's own words) "believing in a Jesus who has saved everyone in principle but never gets close enough to unsettle anyone in particular," well, you may as well leave him in the tomb.

When you do the hard stop here in Mark, when you stop in the harder place... "*They said nothing to anyone, for they were afraid...*" When you stop right there, all you have to hold onto is the promise of God, the promise of God in the words of the young man in a white robe. "*He has been raised; he is not here....he is going ahead of you to Galilee, there you will see him, just has he told you."* As Professor Juel concluded, "The Gospel that ends with frightened women is far more real and holds considerably greater promise." This is because the only one to finish the story is not a scribe, or a Bible editor, or the women or the disciples, or the first century church, or even you and me; the only one who can finish the story is God, because it's God's promise.

"He is going ahead of you ... there you will see him, just as he told you." Or, as the risen Jesus puts it at the end of Matthew's Gospel, *"Go therefore and make disciples of all nations, baptizing them in the name of the Father and of the Son and of the Holy Spirit, and teaching them to obey everything that I have commanded you. And remember, I am with you always, to the end of the age."*

Earlier when we were gathered at the font, I said to Charlotte what I try to say every time we celebrate a Baptism for someone older than an infant, what I try to say to an older sibling standing there with us around the baptismal waters, "Charlotte, this water is a sign that God loves you very, very much. And nothing, nothing, nothing will ever change that." Truth is, I should have said it to Rich, the adult being baptized. "Rich, this water, it's a sign that God loves you very, very much. And nothing, nothing, nothing will ever change that." I should have said it to him. We should say it to parents when they stand up here. We should say it to any witnesses. We should say it over and over again. It is the baptismal promise of God. The prior promise of God. The promise of God we claim in Baptism. *I am with you always.* The baptismal resurrection promise of God. *You will see him just as he told you. I am with you always, to the end of the age.*

The prior promise of God. Not you will win the game, or you will make lots of money, or you will live a long and happy life, or you will be cancer free, or it will be all good all the time, or your most important relationships will always thrive, or your boss will always like you, or you will get in wherever you apply, or you will have no doubts, or you will always have a mountaintop belief, or that all of this (life, meaning, purpose, kingdom, servanthood, following Jesus) is going to be that easy. No. How about *"You will see him just as he told you,"* and *"I will be with you always."*

The baptismal promise of God. That Jesus of Nazareth, the One who brought the kingdom of heaven near, the One who embodied the unconditional love of God, the One who sowed visions of righteousness and snipped away at religiosity, the One who emptied himself and was obedient to the point of death on the cross all the while saying that he would rise again, the Son of God, the Messiah, the Savior, the risen Christ; nothing, nothing, absolutely nothing will ever take his love away from you. He will be with you until the end of the age.

When the women got to the empty tomb, he wasn't there. And at that moment, all they had to go on was a promise. Of course they were scared, and said nothing to anyone. But the story continues, the Gospel continues with the promise of God. The baptismal resurrection promise of God. And those first women, and then the disciples, and then the early church, and then our forebearers in faith, and then you and me…the Living God invites us all to respond to that promise, to live that promise, to participate in that promise, and to carry out that promise with our lives, seeing the risen Jesus there and knowing that with every step, with every day, with every breath and then some, he is with us and for us.

"They said nothing to anyone, for they were afraid." It's a hard stop. Last Sunday, with the sanctuary overflowing and the brass playing and everyone waiting to sing "Thine is the Glory," here's how it should be proclaimed. Here's how to do Easter morning and the end of Mark's Gospel: the congregation is of course all revved up to hear about the risen Jesus. They're ready for "Christ is risen!" Someone stands up to read the Gospel lesson, and stops at v. 8 then sits down. *"They said nothing to anyone, for they were afraid."* Then, nothing. No sermon. No singing. No organ. No brass. No timpani. Only silence and a church full of uncomfortable, shuffling folks wondering what on earth is coming next. What comes next, what breaks that awkward loud silence, the next thing to be spoken, heard…

I Baptize you in the name of the Father, and of the Son, and of the Holy Spirit.

Responding to God's promise and continuing God's story with the discipleship of our lives.

"Idle Tales"

Luke 24:1-12
Easter III

*But on the first day of the week, at early dawn, they
came to the tomb, taking the spices that they had
prepared. They found the stone rolled away from the
tomb, but when they went in, they did not find the body.
While they were perplexed about this, suddenly two
men in dazzling clothes stood beside them. The women
were terrified and bowed their faces to the ground,
but the men said to them, "Why do you look for the
living among the dead? He is not here, but has risen.
Remember how he told you, while he was still in Galilee,
that the Son of Man must be handed over to sinners,
and be crucified, and on the third day rise again?" Then
they remembered his words, and returning from the
tomb, they told all this to the eleven and to all the rest.
Now it was Mary Magdalene, Joanna, Mary the mother
of James, and the other women with them who told this
to the apostles. But these words seemed to them an
idle tale, and they did not believe them. But Peter got
up and ran to the tomb; stooping and looking in, he
saw the linen cloths by themselves; then he went home,
amazed at what had happened.*

It is one of the most disconcerting experiences for a
pastor. The local funeral home calls the church and asks
if the pastor would be available to do a service there
in the funeral home later in the week. The family has

no church home. The person who died had no church affiliation. They would like to have the service Thursday morning at 11:00 A.M. Officiating at a funeral for someone in the community for a family who the minister doesn't know, that's not the disconcerting part. That happens all the time. As a young pastor in South Jersey, I did more than my share. I did so many that, one Christmas, the funeral director gave me one of the matching ties that all the staff would wear when they worked a large funeral. A service for a non-church member is not the challenge. The challenge comes during the service. In the intimate setting of the funeral home, the family is just steps away in the front row, and all that separates the minister is the skinny lectern with the light and the pull chain. The most disconcerting part comes before the eulogy. It comes when Scripture is being read.

The clergy person is reading what is read pretty much at every service. *I lift mine eyes to the hills, from when does my help come.* (Psalm 121) *The Lord is my shepherd, I shall not want.* (Ps 23) *Behold, I tell you a mystery; we shall not all die but we shall be changed.* (I Cor 15) *In my Father's house are many mansions.* (John 14) And somewhere right about, *Thy rod and Thy staff, they comfort me*, the pastor looks up to make eye contact. That's how she was taught. That's how she practiced. And right in that moment she looks into the face of a family member who has absolutely no idea what on earth she is talking about, what she is reading, what crazy stuff she is saying. The stare back has a bit of anger, maybe some disdain, and of course, sorrow. To call it the look of disbelief is probably assuming too much. It's more like a look of someone who has absolutely never heard any of it before, any of what is being read. It makes the pastor feel like she is speaking an unfamiliar language.

That unforgettable disconcerting look, now seared into the pastor's memory, may as well say that you're speaking gibberish or nonsense.

A look something like that must have been what the women saw on the faces of the apostles. *"These words seemed to them an idle tale, and they did not believe them."* An idle tale. Translated in other versions as "nonsense," "pure nonsense." The men thought that this was pure nonsense, even though the women had been to the tomb. An idle tale.

In the sermon two weeks ago on Easter morning, I recounted that, in Matthew's account of the empty tomb, "fear is the only thing mentioned more than the rising of Jesus. Last week in Mark, the hard stop in the Easter morning text was *"They said nothing to anyone, for they were afraid."* What is striking, then, about Luke's account, is that there isn't much fear. When the women found the stone rolled away, when they went in and did not find the body, Luke records that they were perplexed. When the two men suddenly appeared in dazzling clothes and stood right beside them, the women were, of course, terrified. Who wouldn't be? They bowed their faces to the ground, but Luke doesn't say another word about their fear. And the two men, their first words to the women, those first words remarkably were NOT "Do not be afraid." That's what angels are supposed to say. There is no call and response here in Luke about fear. *"Why do you look for the living among the dead? He is not here, but has risen."* Yes, they were afraid, but apparently not afraid enough for the two men to offer the angels' signature words of comfort. When you read the first Easter morning Gospel texts three weeks in a row, it is striking how little fear there is in Luke.

The only thing mentioned more than Jesus being raised in Luke's account of the empty tomb is remembering. *"'Why do you look for the living among the dead? He is not here, but has risen. Remember how he told you, while he was still in Galilee, that the Son of Man must be handed over to sinners, and be crucified, and on the third day rise again?' Then they remembered his words…"* Remember how he told you? Then they remembered. Luke's brief plot of the empty tomb turns on remembering. It is in their remembering that Luke names the women: Mary Magdalene, Joanna, Mary the mother of James, and the others. Named not right at the outset on their way to the tomb, but named in their remembering. It is in their remembering that *"they told all this to the eleven and to all the rest."* Remembering. It's hard to miss in Luke. And when the apostles thought the women were just spouting pure nonsense, when Luke tells the reader they did not believe them, it wasn't just that they didn't believe, it was that they didn't remember. The apostles didn't remember how and what and why he told them. The looks on their faces, must have shown what they were thinking, that what they were hearing was pure nonsense. But the women…they remembered.

You remember that recurrent theme in all the Gospels, how Jesus would teach about his suffering, his death, his resurrection and the disciples wouldn't listen, wouldn't get it? Just here in Luke, Jesus spoke with clarity about what was going to happen to the Son of Man, and he followed up with, *"If any want to become my followers, let them deny themselves and take up their cross daily and follow me."* Then just a bit later in Luke, after Jesus heals a boy and gives him back to his father, after Luke writes that *"All were astounded at the greatness of God,"* Jesus repeated that teaching about his suffering and betrayal. Right then the disciples started to argue about which one of them was the greatest. Again, still in Luke, Jesus took the twelve aside and was very specific about the Son of Man being mocked, insulted, spat upon, flogged, killed ... and that he would rise again on the third day. They understood nothing. It was hidden from them, Luke tells. What happened next was Jesus restoring the sight of the blind man sitting by the side of the road.

In Luke, and in all the Gospels for that matter, Jesus' telling the disciples, teaching the disciples, and predicting his suffering, death, and resurrection is so interwoven with the unfolding Gospel witness to his life, his identity, his relationship to them, his teaching, his actions, his every move. *"Remember how he told you, while he was still in Galilee...."* Remember it, remember all of it. This is not simply remembering the algebraic equation learned for an exam. This is not just remembering one more thing on the list before you leave the store. This is not just remembering the name of that person at work when you see them across the way in the restaurant. And honestly, it's a whole lot more than just remembering 'handed over, crucified, risen on the third day' (A + B = C ... Oh! Check). It wasn't just that they didn't remember what he told them, they weren't remembering him at all! All of him.

These words seemed to the apostles to be pure nonsense. An idle tale. The Greek word here, the one word for idle tale, is unique in the Gospels. This is the only time it is used. The word *idle*, as in resting, or not in use, or unemployed, occurs elsewhere in scripture with a different Greek word. Here, the Greek dictionary translates the word as idle talk, or nonsense. It was like those first proclaimers of the resurrection were speaking gibberish, an unknown language. The apostles and their not remembering, not believing was a singularly unique occurrence, distinctive not just in word choice but in their striking, fleeting yet unforgettable paralysis of remembering, living, acting, in response to the Gospel of Jesus Christ. For in that moment, there was nothing. This was the apostles, and it was if they had never heard any of it before.

That moment in Luke's account of the empty tomb, the apostles' moment of unbelief, wasn't even what public figures today call "misremembering." It was un-remembering. You pretty much can't get any further away from what Jesus of Nazareth told his followers to do. *"Do this in remembrance of me."* Before that walk along the Emmaus Road when the risen Jesus came near and went with them, before he interpreted to them *"all the things about himself in all the scriptures,"* before he *"took bread, blessed, and broke it, and gave it to them,"* before *"their eyes were opened and they recognized him,"* before the risen Christ made himself known to them, to the others, to the church, to you and to me, there was that unforgettable moment of nothingness. And it ought to haunt and inspire, chill and motivate, challenge and exhort any and all who think that the biggest threat to a life in Christ is whether or not you can fathom the resurrection. No, without question, what tears at the life of faith, what eats away at the kingdom, what must cause the most upset in the heart of God is the lingering paralysis of remembering, living, acting, responding to the Gospel of Jesus Christ. To proclaim Christ is risen! He is risen, indeed! And then to do nothing.

Near the end of her book, *Take This Bread: The Spiritual Memoir of a Twenty-First Century Christian,* Sara Miles tells, in uncomfortable detail, the challenge of caring for a dear, dear friend who was dying. With beautiful images of the Lord's Supper, she compares preparing and giving some toast and a glass of water to preparing and offering the Sacrament. The words of the Communion liturgy come to her mind as she is there in the kitchen making toast, breaking bread. In that moment, she finds herself comforted in the presence of the risen Christ. Or as she writes, "I wasn't alone. This wasn't the end." And in giving the toast, she said, "Millie, this is for you." Knowing that Millie wasn't alone either. Then Sara Miles writes about driving across the bridge to home, stunned and blinking and saying aloud to herself in the car, "Oh my God, it's real." What she meant was that, yes, the promise of the Sacrament is real. What she meant was that, yes, the presence of the risen Christ is real. What she meant was that yes, God with us is real. "I wasn't alone. This wasn't the end." The risen Christ present and made real in her caring for the dying, and offering love and compassion in the most human, ordinary, and remarkably holy of ways.

She was remembering.

"I am the Resurrection, and I am Life"

EASTER IV

Early on the first day of the week, while it was still dark, Mary Magdalene came to the tomb and saw that the stone had been removed from the tomb. So she ran and went to Simon Peter and the other disciple, the one whom Jesus loved, and said to them, "They have taken the Lord out of the tomb, and we do not know where they have laid him." Then Peter and the other disciple set out and went toward the tomb. The two were running together, but the other disciple outran Peter and reached the tomb first. He bent down to look in and saw the linen wrappings lying there, but he did not go in. Then Simon Peter came, following him, and went into the tomb. He saw the linen wrappings lying there, and the cloth that had been on Jesus' head, not lying with the linen wrappings but rolled up in a place by itself. Then the other disciple, who reached the tomb first, also went in, and he saw and believed; for as yet they did not understand the Scripture, that he must rise from the dead. Then the disciples returned to their homes.

But Mary stood weeping outside the tomb. As she wept, she bent over to look into the tomb; and she saw two angels in white, sitting where the body of Jesus had been lying, one at the head and the other at the feet. They said to her, "Woman, why are you weeping?" She said to them, "They have taken away my Lord, and I do not know where they have laid him." When she had said this, she turned around and saw Jesus standing there, but she did not know that it was Jesus. Jesus said to her,

"Woman, why are you weeping? Whom are you looking for?" Supposing him to be the gardener, she said to him, "Sir, if you have carried him away, tell me where you have laid him, and I will take him away." Jesus said to her, "Mary!" She turned and said to him in Hebrew, "Rabbouni!" (which means 'Teacher'). Jesus said to her, "Do not hold on to me, because I have not yet ascended to the Father. But go to my brothers and say to them, 'I am ascending to my Father and your Father, to my God and your God.'" Mary Magdalene went and announced to the disciples, "I have seen the Lord"; and she told them that he had said these things to her.

Like many parents, I have often found myself channeling the voice of one my own parents as I dished out profound advice and wisdom to my own children. One's awareness of the generativity of parental teaching can be a bit frightening. When one of our kids was banged up on the field and I would yell "run it out:" that was my father's voice coming through me. Just like this one, "You might be able to stay out later, but the car still has an 11:00 curfew." My mother's advice on love and dating: "Never touch skin to skin." I've only said that one a few times. And this classic from my mother, and I bet from many others over the generations, maybe yours as well, "Nothing good happens after midnight." Or some variation: "Nothing good happens when you're out after midnight. Be extra careful when you're on the road, after midnight. After midnight, it's not you I worry about, it's everyone else." Age-old wisdom about life when it's really dark out.

I took a group of men from my first congregation to spend the weekend at our cabin in the Endless Mountains of Sullivan County, Pennsylvania. It wasn't a retreat. These guys brought all their tools, and we worked on the cabin. Given my skill level for such things, they tired quickly of teaching me and I mostly made the sandwich and beer runs. At the end of a long day, the lights were out and we were all tucked in for the night in sleeping bags. One the guys said, "It is so dark in here." It was rather obvious. But then he said, "It is darker with my eyes open than it is with my eyes closed." That's really dark.

In the Gospel of John, soon after Jesus spoke those unforgettable words in the 3rd chapter, *"For God so loved the world that he gave his only Son ... ,"* just after that promise, that memory verse, Jesus said, *"This is the judgment, that the light has come into the world and the people loved darkness rather than light because their deeds were evil."* People loved darkness rather than light. You remember that the Lord's teaching here comes in response to Nicodemus. It's the same section of the Gospel where Jesus speaks about being born again: *"Very truly I tell you, no one can see the kingdom of God without being born from above."* According to John, the Pharisee Nicodemus came to Jesus by night. That teaching about seeing the kingdom, and the judgment that people loved darkness, all happened in the dark.

Jesus said, *"Those who walk during the day do not stumble, because they see the light of this world. But those who walk at night stumble, because the light is not in them."* That's in John. *"I have come as light into the world, so that everyone who believes in me should not remain in darkness."* Jesus said that in John. *"What has come into being in him was life, and the life was the light of all people. The light shines in the darkness, and the darkness did not overcome it."* The prologue in John. And as Fleming Rutledge, the Episcopal preacher, points out, when Jesus called out Judas as the one who would betray him, when Jesus dipped a piece of bread and gave it to Judas, as the Bible says, Satan entered him after he received that bread. After he received the bread, Judas went out. And the Gospel writer John puts an exclamation point on it for the reader. John writes: *"And it was night."* Everyone assumes that Last Supper/Garden/betrayal scene occurred at night. Everyone sort of figures, including the other Gospel writers. But not John, he has to underline it for you. When it comes to Judas, and betraying, and Satan, and *"Do quickly what you are going to do,"* John has to underline the darkness.

So, when the church finally gets to Easter morning, and John writes that *"Early on the first day of the week, while it was still dark, Mary Magdalene came to the tomb,"* you ought not to miss that, or take it for granted, the *"while it was still dark"* part. The other three Gospels are very clear that Easter starts at the break of day: "As the first day of the week was dawning" (Matthew), "Very early on the first day of the week, when the sun had risen" (Mark), and "On the first day of the week, at early dawn" (Luke). But not John, *"Early on the first day of the week, while it was still dark, Mary Magdalene came to the tomb."* Still dark. That's really dark. Nothing good happens when it's really dark out.

Clearly, darkness in John has little to do with the time of day. Darkness has everything to do with all that is opposite to the mighty works of God. All the powers and principalities that work to destroy life; life in all fullness as Jesus said in John. Darkness; the symbol, the sum, the prototype, the theme, the weight, the rallying cry in John for all that works against God, God's Reign, God's kingdom. In John, Jesus said, *"I am the bread of life, I am the vine you are the branches, I am the gate, I am the good shepherd, I am the light of the world, I am the way, the truth, and the life, I am the resurrection and I am the life."* Essentially, Jesus was saying, "I am all of this….and that, that is darkness. Darkness is death." *"Early on the first day of the week, while it was still dark, Mary Magdalene came to the tomb."*

This isn't dark as when a theater or concert hall is empty for the evening with nothing scheduled, "the hall is dark." This isn't dark as when you are at the theater for an Anton Chekhov play that is so depressing and there's so much yelling that you consider leaving at intermission, saying to your seatmate, "It's too dark." This is the kind of dark that comes amid the bright lights of a hospital waiting room, when 'butterflies in your stomach' doesn't begin to describe it, and as you wait for the doctor, you keep trying to tell yourself this is all a dream and this can't be happening. This is the kind of dark that tomorrow brings when it takes absolutely every ounce of courage you have to stay sober today. The dark that comes when your grandchild tells you about the mean kids at school and you can't find any words to make him feel better. The dark that comes as the person you love like no other names her infidelity. When you take that walk from the car to the grave in the cemetery you always thought was so beautiful, or when you're the one making the walk because of the absolute finality and boundless reach of death. Sometimes it's just darker when your eyes are open.

According to John, the resurrection happened in the dead of night, while it was still dark. John Calvin minimizes the whole dark vs. morning light issue, choosing to argue that Mary started out from home when it was still dark. As indicated by the other Gospels, it would have been daybreak by the time she got there. No, it was dark. Jesus rose from the dead when it was really dark; before she got there, before they got there, before anyone got there. That resurrection, promise-fulfilling, salvific, earth-shattering moment. It was dark and no one was there but Jesus and God. There's an intimacy to his resurrection. No trumpet blast, no proclamation. Just Jesus and God and the dark. I wonder what Jesus said to God when it was just the two of them. Clearly, they talked all the time. The last thing Jesus said in John was, "It is finished!" After his eyes popped open and he drew a breath. His face covered, his body wrapped. Inside a tomb, by the way, that would have been the very definition of dark. I can't imagine that he said in some royal third person fashion, "He is risen!" There in the utter darkness, in a tomb of all places, where death slams the door forever, there was just God and Jesus. Jesus must have at least said, "Yes," for the victory was his. The victory was theirs. The victory is ours. He either said, "Yes," or he repeated what he said the last time he stood at a tomb. But if he said it this time, he said it only to God, to himself, and he said as he spit at the darkness, "*I am the resurrection, and I am the life.*"

One of the most influential preachers in my life once said this in a sermon on Easter morning:

> *Ours is a religion of the dawn. Creation begins in the morning. The women come to the tomb in the morning. The morning is when it happens. Lose the morning and you have lost the day. Resurrection is an event of the morning, and when Jesus is raised*

*from the dead it is always morning, always day-
time, always the new day....The theme of Easter is
that you and I become something new. We are given
a second chance to get it right.*

With all due respect to a mentor now gone to glory, if
the theme of Easter is just a second chance to get it
right, if Easter is just one big mulligan, one big do-over
for humankind, that's not enough. Because you and I,
humankind, the world, we will never get it right. Before
the resurrection is an event of the morning, it is a death-
vanquishing, life-restoring, tomb-stomping, event in the
dark. It's a light breaking, shattering, overcoming of the
dark. *"Early on the first day of the week, while it was still
dark, Mary Magdalene came to the tomb."*

I have stood here before and admitted to turning to ESPN
at the end of the day to avoid the world's darkness trum-
peted by way of the news. My response to the coverage
of the events in Baltimore after the death of Freddy Gray
has been quite different. I have found myself reading and
listening more rather than less; the cable coverage, the
pundits lining up like lawyers, the people who find their
way to every camera or microphone, jousting editorials in
print from the *New York Times* and the *Wall Street Journal*,
or other various blog posts, online essays, and interviews.
But once again, I made a rookie mistake when it comes to
reading about current events online. I made the unfortu-
nate mistake of reading responses posted below the blog,
below the article. Oh my goodness. Those anonymous
postings, the discussions, and the hate that comes from
all sides is like a 21st century version of the crowd that
shouted, "Crucify him, crucify him!" Talk about a window
to humanity's dark side. God help us! Easter better be

about more than a second chance. Second chances aren't enough when you're talking about all that is opposite to the mighty works of God. All the powers and principalities that work to destroy life in all fullness. Second chances aren't enough when it comes to the symbol, the sum, the prototype, the theme, the weight, the rallying cry for all that works against God, God's Reign, God's kingdom. When confronted over and over again by such utter darkness, it's not a second chance I need, but rather the hope, the promise, the God-given Word of a victory. God's "Yes."

Don't misunderstand; I have no illusions when it comes to death. I've stood next to far too many open graves. Death and darkness abound and are very, very real. But the promise of everlasting life; yes. The hope that death and darkness will be no more; yes. That there will be no need of light there; for God alone shall be our light; yes. That in the kingdom that comes here on earth as it is in heaven, that gun violence and bitterness, and the evils of fear and hate will be no more; yes. That the city of Jerusalem, and all that is the land of Jesus' birth, would have a future of peace; yes. The earth could live free forever from weapons of mass destruction and the inevitability of war; yes. That abundant life can rise out of the shambles of broken relationships, and a flourishing career can come after the depth of job loss, and youthful vitality can rise from weak knees and tired bones and weary souls; yes. That the brightest of futures can come from the most brutal of college acceptance and rejection, that a fruitful ministry will rise out of a failed ordination exam, that a community of faith called to this room over and over again by death would be bold enough to witness and celebrate life; yes. That, as an Easter people, the people of God would rise not just celebrating a second chance, but rise to stare down the world's darkness, proclaiming together that the victory was his, the victory is ours; yes.

While it was still dark, Jesus opened his eyes, took a breath, and said, "Yes."

www.ingramcontent.com/pod-product-compliance
Lightning Source LLC
Chambersburg PA
CBHW071235090426
42736CB00014B/3087